THE COMPLETE GUIDE TO
BLENDED LEARNING

ACTIVATING AGENCY, DIFFERENTIATION, COMMUNITY, AND INQUIRY FOR STUDENTS

CATLIN R. TUCKER

Solution Tree | Press

555 North Morton Street
Bloomington, IN 47404
800.733.6786 (toll free) / 812.336.7700
FAX: 812.336.7790

email: info@SolutionTree.com
SolutionTree.com

Visit **go.SolutionTree.com/technology** to download the free reproducibles in this book.

Printed in the United States of America

Library of Congress Cataloging-in-Publication Data

Names: Tucker, Catlin R., author.
Title: The complete guide to blended learning : activating agency,
   differentiation, community, and inquiry for students / Catlin R. Tucker.
Description: Bloomington : Solution Tree Press, [2022] | Includes
   bibliographical references and index.
Identifiers: LCCN 2021058327 (print) | LCCN 2021058328 (ebook) | ISBN
   9781954631335 (paperback) | ISBN 9781954631342 (ebook)
Subjects: LCSH: Blended learning. | Educational technology. | Web-based
   instruction.
Classification: LCC LB1028.5 .T7643 2022 (print) | LCC LB1028.5 (ebook) |
   DDC 371.3--dc23/eng/20220106
LC record available at https://lccn.loc.gov/2021058327
LC ebook record available at https://lccn.loc.gov/2021058328

Solution Tree
Jeffrey C. Jones, CEO
Edmund M. Ackerman, President

Solution Tree Press
President and Publisher: Douglas M. Rife
Associate Publisher: Sarah Payne-Mills
Managing Production Editor: Kendra Slayton
Editorial Director: Todd Brakke
Art Director: Rian Anderson
Copy Chief: Jessi Finn
Production Editor: Miranda Addonizio
Content Development Specialist: Amy Rubenstein
Acquisitions Editor: Sarah Jubar
Proofreader: Sarah Ludwig
Text Designer: Kelsey Hoover
Cover Designer: Fabiana Cochran
Associate Editor: Sarah Ludwig
Editorial Assistants: Charlotte Jones and Elijah Oates

For my children, Cheyenne and Maddox, you have been my most powerful teachers. You inspired me and my work. I feel grateful every day to be your mom.

ACKNOWLEDGMENTS

Solution Tree Press would like to thank the following reviewers:

Lety Amalla
Executive Director of Student
Programs
Midland ISD
Midland, Texas

Racquel Biem
High School Teacher
Saskatchewan Teachers Federation
Swift Current, Saskatchewan

Charles Ames Fischer
Education Consultant
Decatur, Tennessee

Justin Green
Third-Grade Teacher
Nanaimo Ladysmith Public Schools
Nanaimo, British Columbia

Chris Hansen
Director of Learning
Hortonville Area School District
Greenville, Wisconsin

Peter Marshall
Education Consultant and Trainer
Recently Retired Principal
Burlington, Ontario, Canada

Jen Minor
Administrative Leadership
Deer Valley Unified School District
Phoenix, Arizona

Paige Raney
Chair, Division of Education
Spring Hill College
Mobile, Alabama

Sarah Carson Svendsen
Kindergarten Teacher, Instructional
Coach

Ringnolda Jofee' Tremain
PK3–8 Principal
Trinity Basin Preparatory
Fort Worth, Texas

Britney Watson
Principal
Fort Smith Public Schools, Morrison
Elementary School
Fort Smith, Arkansas

Allison Zamarripa
Reading and Language Arts
Curriculum and Instructional Specialist
Pasadena Independent School District
Pasadena, Texas

TABLE OF CONTENTS

Reproducibles are in italics.

ABOUT THE AUTHOR

Catlin R. Tucker, EdD, is a best-selling author, keynote speaker, international trainer, and professor in the master of arts in teaching program at Pepperdine University in California. She taught for sixteen years in Sonoma County, California, where she was named Teacher of the Year in 2010.

Catlin has written several books on blended learning, including *Blended Learning in Grades 4–12*, *Blended Learning in Action*, *Power Up Blended Learning, Balance With Blended Learning*, and *UDL and Blended Learning: Thriving in Flexible Learning Landscapes*. In addition to her books on blended learning, Catlin writes an internationally ranked blog and hosts a podcast called *The Balance*.

Catlin earned her bachelor of arts degree in English literature from the University of California at Los Angeles. She earned her English credential and master's degree in education at the University of California at Santa Barbara. In 2020, Catlin earned her doctorate in learning technologies at Pepperdine University, researching teacher engagement in blended learning environments.

To learn more about Catlin's work, visit https://CatlinTucker.com or follow @Catlin _Tucker on Twitter.

INTRODUCTION

I entered the teaching profession at the age of twenty-two excited to actualize the classroom I had been fantasizing about since I began my credential program at the University of California in Santa Barbara. While studying to become a teacher, I dreamed about my future classroom. I imagined my students bounding through the door, eager and excited to learn. I pictured them sitting in circles, talking animatedly about literature and life. And as you may guess, the reality of my first few years in this profession stood in stark contrast to these elaborate fantasies. Instead of bounding through the door, my students trudged. Instead of engaging in conversation, they slumped in their chairs, avoiding eye contact. They were not excited to be at school generally or in my class specifically. It did not take long for me to become exhausted and disillusioned with teaching. These feelings stemmed from the realization that I was failing. I was failing to create the classroom I had dreamed about. I was failing to engage my students in dynamic learning experiences. I began to worry that I had made a huge mistake by becoming a teacher.

My career crisis aligned with my decision to have my first child. I decided to take a year off from my teaching position to be home with my daughter. About six months into my tenure as a stay-at-home mom, I began teaching online college-level writing courses. Before my experience as an online professor, I would not have described myself as interested in technology, much less technology savvy. However, my experience teaching entirely online piqued my interest in the potential benefits of using technology to engage learners.

When I returned to my high school classroom, I was determined to give the teaching profession one more year. I decided to treat my classroom like a laboratory and experiment with some of the online learning strategies I'd become familiar with while teaching my online college classes. *What did I have to lose?* It was 2008, and my public high school was low-tech. However, the emergence of the iPhone in 2007 had set off an explosion of handheld devices and smartphones that began to appear on campus and in my classroom. I had to leverage the handful of devices that came through the door in my students' pockets. At first, I had maybe four students of thirty-plus who had a smartphone. By 2010, more than half my class had them. In those early years, devices were limited, so everything my students did with technology required conversation and collaboration as they shared devices.

The results of my experimentation were nothing short of magical. I began to reimagine my role in the learning process, slowly shifting the focus away from myself in the design and facilitation of lessons. I didn't need to have all the answers or supply all the information. Instead, I challenged students to ask and answer their own questions—to investigate, explore, make meaning, and work together to create artifacts of their learning that *they* were proud of. A few months into this experimentation, I had manifested the classroom I had dreamed about in credential school. Students were engaging in conversations, leaning into the learning, and taking risks.

> I didn't need to have all the answers or supply all the information. Instead, I challenged students to ask and answer their own questions—to investigate, explore, and make meaning, and work together to create artifacts of their learning that *they* were proud of.

I learned many powerful lessons from my early work weaving together offline and online learning. It forced me to reevaluate my true value in the classroom. Instead of feeling pressure to be the expert in everything, I began to let go and allow my students to develop their own expertise. I spent less time at the front of the room transferring information and telling students everything I knew about a topic or a text. I spent more time working with small groups of learners or individual students to support them as they developed their content knowledge and honed specific skills. I realized that my value was not tied up in my content-area expertise but rather in my ability to connect with learners. I embraced my role as a facilitator and coach, designing learning experiences that allowed me to spend more time engaged in the human work of making connections that is critical to learning. If you are scared that technology will replace you, you can put that worry aside; it won't. Technology cannot replace the human side of the work we do as teachers, and that is where our actual value lies.

My success with this mix of online and offline learning has made me a passionate advocate for blended learning, which combines online and offline learning to give students more control over how they learn. Shifting from a traditional, teacher-centered approach to a blended, student-centered design transformed my classroom and my relationships with students. There is research to show that my experience is not unique (Kazakoff, Macaruso, & Hook, 2018; Pegrum, Oakley, & Faulkner, 2013; Turner, Young-Lowe, & Newton, 2018; Truitt & Ku, 2018).

Although I have written extensively about blended learning, this book was inspired by my work supporting teachers during the early stages of the COVID-19 pandemic. Teachers all over the world were expected to use technology and navigate online learning with little preparation. I wanted to write a comprehensive book on blended learning that would pull together my years of experience and research to provide teachers with a complete guide to support them in using technology not just to survive the challenges of teaching in a pandemic but also to engage learners, enhance the student learning experience, and thrive in the teaching profession.

This book provides specific strategies to implement blended learning, includes reproducible templates, incorporates reflection and discussion questions, and challenges teachers to apply their learning with hands-on tasks. The goal of this book is to provide educators with a solid foundation on which to begin their blended learning journeys. While it's ideal as a starting point for those new to blended learning, the tools and strategies I present here are useful for educators at any stage of implementation. Many educators are using technology in classrooms, but they may not be using that technology to give students agency, differentiate and personalize the learning experience, or shift control from teacher to learner. Although these teachers may feel they are already using blended learning, they and their students are not experiencing its true potential. This book will support teachers in designing and facilitating blended learning experiences that aim to position students at the center of the learning experience.

> I embraced my role as a facilitator and coach, designing learning experiences that allowed me to spend more time engaged in the human work of making connections that is so critical to learning. If you are scared that technology will replace you, you can put that worry aside; it won't. Technology cannot replace the human side of the work we do as teachers, and that is where our actual value lies.

The COVID-19 pandemic has made it clear that educators must cultivate a mindset, skill set, and toolset that allow them to navigate flexible learning landscapes. This book provides a clear path forward that effectively blends the best aspects of offline and online learning. That way teachers have the confidence and self-efficacy to thrive in class, online, or a blend of the two. Before diving in, I will explain a little more about the book and its organization, go over the theoretical framework that provides its foundation, and wrap up with some reflection questions and next steps.

About This Book

This book provides a clear understanding of what blended learning is and how to design and facilitate learning experiences that shift the focus from the teacher to the learners.

Education, like all aspects of our lives, is heavily impacted by technology. This can be exciting if you know how to harness the power of technology to enhance learning. Incorporating technology strategically into a learning environment should create more opportunities for students to drive their experience and free you to work directly with learners. Additionally, it can help you feel more confident blending online and offline learning to give students more agency, differentiate and personalize learning, and shift control over the pace of learning to the students. These aspects of blended learning have the potential to dramatically improve both the teacher and student experience.

Let's take a quick look at who this book is for and how schools can use it as well as how it's organized.

Who This Book Is For

This book is for K–12 teachers, school leaders, administrators, instructional coaches, teacher training programs, and collaborative teams who want to begin their blended learning journeys. You can incorporate the strategies I present in this book across grade levels and content areas; however, I do not attempt to provide specific examples for every grade level or content area.

Blended learning provides *all* teachers with a path to create learning experiences that allow for small-group and individual instruction. This approach makes it more manageable for teachers in early elementary to support small groups in developing foundational skills, since students enter kindergarten with a wide range of skills, abilities, and language proficiencies. Similarly, secondary teachers can leverage blended learning models to differentiate effectively, challenging students where they are in their individual learning journeys by providing meaningful choices and flexible pathways.

Leaders and instructional coaches can use this book to understand the shifts taking place in classrooms as teachers transition from traditional, whole-group instruction to blended learning models. It's critical that school leaders and instructional coaches know what to look for when entering classrooms to conduct observations or provide feedback. Additionally, coaches can use the strategies, templates, and examples in this book when working with teachers to design lessons using the various blended learning models.

At the school level, educators can use this book for a campuswide book study, pairing experienced staff members with strong content knowledge and experience with newer staff members who may be more proficient with technology, thus allowing them to learn from each other's strengths. Departments, teaching teams, or schools functioning as professional learning communities (PLCs) can use this book as a resource in their continued professional learning. The chapter-ending questions are designed to spark reflection and discussion about the content and strategies, while the next steps encourage educators to act on what they are learning. Implementing blended learning benefits immensely from the support and feedback of colleagues.

How This Book Is Organized

Chapter 1 defines *blended learning,* grounding it in a constructivist perspective—that is, the assumption that learners construct knowledge as opposed to absorbing information. I describe the purpose, value, and benefits of a shift to blended learning. I also review a revised taxonomy of blended learning models with an emphasis on the rotation models, which will be the focus of this book because they work well in a traditional school setting, online, or a blend of the two.

Chapter 2 focuses on building a technology toolbox for a blended learning environment. We'll explore the following.

- The role of the learning management system (LMS)
- Leveraging technology tools to prioritize the four Cs of 21st century learning: (1) critical thinking, (2) communication, (3) collaboration, and (4) creativity (Partnership for 21st Century Learning, 2019)
- Using the substitution, augmentation, modification, redefinition (SAMR) framework (Puentedura, 2013) as a guide to self-assess our technology use

Chapters 3 through 7 are organized using the three dimensions of the community of inquiry (COI) framework: (1) the teaching presence, (2) the social presence, and (3) the cognitive presence (Garrison, Anderson, & Archer, 1999, 2001, 2010). Chapters 3 through 5 cover the teaching presence, exploring the teacher's roles as designer, instructor, and facilitator in a blended learning environment.

Chapter 3 focuses on the teacher's role as designer in a blended learning environment and provides a deep dive into the mechanics of designing learning experiences using each of the rotation models.

- The station rotation model
- The whole-group rotation model
- The flipped classroom model
- The playlist or individual rotation model

I introduce the structure of each model, discuss the benefits for learners, and provide ideas for how to use these structures to design student-centered learning experiences. Throughout the discussion of each model, I thread three themes: (1) student agency, (2) differentiation, and (3) student control over the pace of learning.

Chapter 4 focuses on the teacher's role as instructor in a blended learning environment. I focus on synchronous, small-group instruction, which occurs in a shared space and time, like a classroom or online class using a video-conferencing platform, and asynchronous, video-based instruction, which occurs at different times because the students can access and view the video anytime from anywhere. They both have a place in a blended learning environment, and this chapter highlights benefits and limitations of each type of instruction. I share strategies for structuring live, small-group instruction, and review best practices for creating video content.

Chapter 5 explores the teacher's role as a facilitator and partner in a blended learning environment. I present strategies and routines designed to support metacognitive skill building, help teachers facilitate academic discourse, allow them to provide timely, actionable feedback, and guide them in structuring teacher-student conferences.

Chapter 6 explores the social presence of the COI, helping teachers cultivate a classroom culture that encourages students to project their social and emotional selves in their interactions in class and online. It focuses on the importance of building a learning community that prioritizes relationships and co-constructs agreements about what participation looks like and what behaviors will keep the learning community feeling safe, respectful, and productive. I share specific strategies you can use to facilitate relationship building among your students so they can feel comfortable taking interpersonal risks. A community built on respect and trust can effectively construct meaning together. I use the Collaborative for Academic, Social, and Emotional Learning (CASEL) social-emotional learning (SEL) framework (CASEL, n.d.) to anchor this conversation about the skills students need to thrive in a blended learning community.

Chapter 7 covers the cognitive presence of the COI and explores how teachers can use the 5E instructional model—(1) engage, (2) explore, (3) explain, (4) elaborate, and (5) evaluate (Bybee, 2014; Bybee et al., 2006)—to blend online and offline elements to design student-centered inquiry around essential questions and encourage the collaborative construction of knowledge. The 5E instructional model aligns with the cognitive presence and its inquiry cycle, and teachers can use it effectively in class, online, or a blend of the two.

Chapter 8 highlights the key mindset shifts necessary for a successful transition to blended learning. I'll review key design and facilitation elements necessary to maximize the effectiveness of blended learning. This chapter provides educators with a path forward to continue building on the fundamentals covered in this book.

At the close of each chapter are reproducible pages with reflection and discussion questions that you can copy or download to use as you wish. Following the final chapter is a glossary of key terms used in the book for easy reference.

The Theoretical Framework That Serves as the Foundation for This Book

The COI theoretical framework, which grounds my work and research on blended learning, serves as the foundation for this book. COI was initially conceived by Canadian researchers D. Randy Garrison, Terry Anderson, and Walter Archer (1999, 2001, 2010) to address the unique nature of teaching and learning online. In COI, students work both individually and collaboratively to construct knowledge by exploring ideas and information, engaging in conversation, collaborating around shared tasks, and reflecting on their learning (Swan, 2019; Vaughan, Cleveland-Innes, & Garrison, 2013). The COI framework places the student at the center of learning as an active agent, emphasizes the value of interaction with a community of learners, and prioritizes inquiry as critical aspects of a learning experience.

The COI, as I mentioned, is composed of three overlapping dimensions, or presences, that work in concert to create a dynamic learning community—(1) the teaching presence, (2) the social presence, and (3) the cognitive presence—as pictured in figure I.1 (page 8). It is the interplay among these three presences, or dimensions, of a community of

> The COI framework places the student at the center of learning as an active agent, emphasizes the value of interaction with a community of learners, and prioritizes inquiry as critical aspects of a learning experience. The COI is grounded in constructivist principles, and it anchors much of the existing research on blended and online learning.

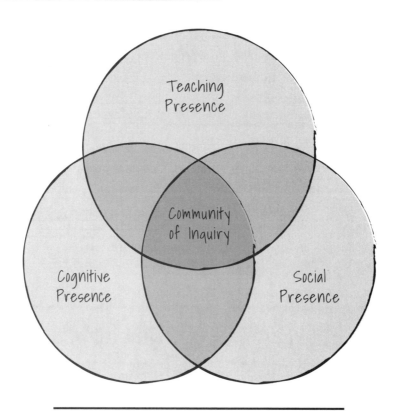

FIGURE I.1: The community of inquiry theoretical framework.

inquiry that creates dynamic blended and online learning experiences that challenge students to work both individually and collectively to make meaning. In order to cultivate a COI, teachers must proactively work to develop strong teaching, social, and cognitive presences in a blended learning environment. Teachers can use this framework to guide their thinking about their roles and the students' role in the learning process.

Teaching Presence

The *teaching presence*, or the teacher's design, facilitation, and direction of the cognitive and social presences in a course to yield high-quality learning, is critical to creating and sustaining a high-functioning learning community (Akyol & Garrison, 2011; Swan, 2019). Think of the teaching presence as the glue holding the three-part structure of the COI together—without it, the social and cognitive aspects of the learning environment would fall apart. The teaching presence encompasses the teacher's roles as designer, instructor, and facilitator, as described in table I.1. Because the teaching presence is so crucial, I have dedicated chapters 3–5 of this book to the three primary roles of teachers in a blended or online learning environment.

Table I.1: The Teaching Presence—Roles and Responsibilities

The Teaching Presence	
Role	Responsibility
Designer	The work teachers do to design student-centered learning experiences that invite the students to make meaning; in a blended learning environment, this requires a high level of intentionality and an understanding of how to utilize and maximize the affordances of each learning landscape—online and offline.
Instructor	The teacher's content-area and pedagogical expertise; this is the work teachers do to transfer information, unpack and explain important concepts, and model specific strategies and skills.
Facilitator	The teacher's guidance of the learning process and coaching of students as they work to ensure they are making progress toward stated learning goals; this includes helping learners develop metacognitive skills, engage in productive conversations, and improve via regular, timely, actionable feedback.

Social Presence

The *social presence* is students' ability to project their social and emotional selves in a blended or online environment (Garrison & Vaughan, 2008; Swan, 2019). To successfully construct knowledge as part of a learning community, students must see their peers as real people, even when they are interacting with each other online. In classes where relationships among students are cultivated and students perceive a strong social presence, students report high levels of engagement, interaction, participation, and perceived learning (Kreijns, Van Acker, Vermeulen, and Van Buuren, 2014). The social presence comprises three dimensions, which include (1) affective expression, (2) open communication, and (3) a sense of group cohesion, as described in table I.2.

Table I.2: The Dimensions of the Social Presence

The Social Presence	
Dimension	Description
Affective Expression	Students' ability and willingness to express their feelings, beliefs, and values in their interactions with peers; this makes it possible for them to interact authentically and honestly with their classmates.
Open Communication	Students' ability and willingness to engage in open and purposeful conversation with their peers; this enables students to explore ideas and work collaboratively to construct meaning as part of a learning community.
Group Cohesion	Students' feeling of connectedness to other members of the learning community; this cohesion is strengthened when learners work together to explore ideas or collaborate on shared tasks.

Cognitive Presence

The *cognitive presence* is students' ability to construct and confirm meaning both through individual processes of exploration and reflection as well as through their interactions and discussions with the other members of the learning community (Breivik, 2016; Garrison et al., 2001). The cognitive presence is grounded in an inquiry cycle comprising the following four stages: (1) triggering event, (2) exploration, (3) integration, and (4) resolution, as pictured in figure I.2.

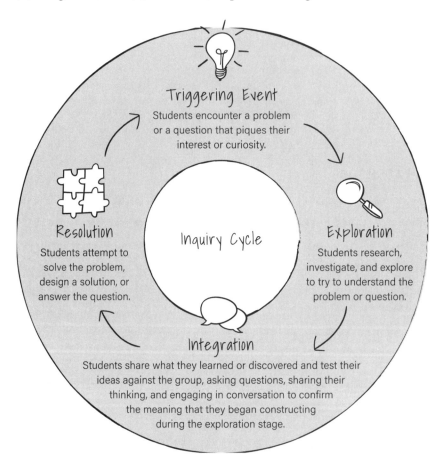

FIGURE I.2: Inquiry cycle at the heart of the cognitive presence.

This inquiry cycle capitalizes on the learner's curiosity and combines both individual and social processes of making meaning (Garrison et al., 2001). During exploration, students work to develop their individual understanding of the the issue, problem, or question at the heart of the inquiry. Then integration brings the members of the learning community together to engage in conversation, testing their understandings and ideas out against the group. Integration is the stage of the inquiry cycle where students learn with and from each other.

Even though the focus of this book is blended learning, successful teachers' mind-sets, skill sets, and toolsets must transcend any single learning landscape. Teachers must be prepared for flexible learning landscapes and have the ability to apply our blended learning knowledge to design an entirely in-class learning experience, as is the case in most elementary classrooms, or an entirely online learning experience, as became necessary during the pandemic in 2020 and is often the case when severe weather strikes. The goal of this book is to help you develop a high level of confidence in your ability to take what you'll learn here and apply it to the teaching environment you are in at any given moment.

Wrap-Up and Next Steps

Learning is an active process. Students need to actively engage with their teachers, their peers, and the content to learn concepts and develop skills. Blended learning strives to position the learner at the center of learning. The COI framework provides a foundation for this book and informs many of the ideas and strategies I present within. You can develop and nurture the teaching, social, and cognitive presences with intention to cultivate a dynamic learning community capable of making meaning together. This book guides teachers in exploring strategies and routines necessary to develop the dimensions of each presence in a blended learning environment. As a complete guide, this book strives to provide all the tools you need to cultivate a dynamic community of inquiry where students are positioned to make meaning on their own and in collaboration with their classmates.

Consider taking the following next steps as a way to further what you've learned. See also the reflection questions on page 12.

- Think about *why* you picked up this book. What is the purpose or value of a shift to blended learning? Take a moment to write a clear why statement articulating the purpose or value of this shift that you can share with your students and their parents or guardians. Your why statement should be inspiring and to the point so you can easily share it with your stakeholders to garner support fo this shift.

- Once you have written your why statement, publish it somewhere. Share it on social media, write it on a poster and hang it in your classroom, or jot it in a planner that you use every day.

Introduction: Reflect and Discuss

As you read this book, I encourage you to pause at the end of each chapter to reflect on or discuss the following questions. If you are reading this book on your own, you can reflect on these questions in a blog post, publish your thoughts on your favorite social media platform, or capture your thoughts in a journal or notebook. If you are reading this book as part of a book club or book study, use the following questions to facilitate vibrant in-person or online discussions. Regardless of the strategy you use, the goal is to get you thinking more deeply about the ideas and strategies presented in this book.

1. Think about your experiences as a learner. How would you describe the most engaging or effective learning experiences you have had as a student? What learning activities or instructional strategies were most effective in helping you learn as a student?

2. Create a Venn diagram comparing and contrasting the attributes and qualities of a teacher-centered classroom with a student-centered classroom. Would you describe your classes as teacher centered or student centered? How might a focus on developing a community of inquiry shift the focus from you to your students?

3. When you think about the three roles and responsibilities described in the teaching presence—(1) designer, (2) instructor, and (3) facilitator—which role do you spend the most time and energy in right now? Why do you spend so much time in this role? Do you enjoy it? Which role do you spend the least time and energy in? Is your current approach allowing you to connect with and support individual and small groups of learners?

4. Which dimension of the social presence do you feel you currently do the best job of cultivating—affective expression, open communication, or group cohesion? What strategies are you currently using to develop this dimension of the social presence?

5. Which dimension of the social presence do you feel you need to spend more time and energy cultivating—affective expression, open communication, or group cohesion? Why do you think this aspect of the social presence has been more challenging to develop?

6. What role does student-centered inquiry play in your class? How do you encourage students to explore and discuss topics, issues, concepts, or questions? How might leveraging an inquiry cycle, like the one described in the section on cognitive presence, impact student interest and engagement?

CHAPTER 1

THE BASICS OF BLENDED LEARNING

Growing up, my interactions with the world were radically different from how my two children expect to engage with the world. When I wanted to listen to music, I had a collection of FM radio stations, and the radio DJ chose the music. As a consumer of media, I had very little control. Sure, I could turn the dial, but my options were limited. Unless I wanted to actually own the albums, I had to listen to what was made available to me.

My children possess the control I lacked. Instead of listening to the radio, they build customized playlists of music on Spotify (www.spotify.com). They are actively creating soundtracks for their lives. They have a collection of songs they listen to when studying and another playlist they listen to when working on their soccer skills in the backyard. They frequently put a track on repeat and play it until I want to lose my mind. They control the content. They personalize the experience.

Given that this level of control over their experience is their norm beyond the classroom, it makes sense why so many students feel increasingly disillusioned with school (Lawson & Lawson, 2020). School may be the one place where they are without control. In many classrooms, the content is the same for everyone, so like it or not, they are all listening to the same metaphorical radio station. They receive information and instructions; they are told what to do and how to do it. This lack of agency over their environment and experience stands in stark contrast to the rest of their lives. If we, as teachers, want students to be engaged at school and interested in their classes, we need to prioritize student agency, personalize the experience, and shift control from teacher to learner. But how do we do that in a way that feels doable and sustainable? I believe blended learning provides a path to do just that.

In this chapter, I unpack blended learning, discuss the purpose or value of shifting to blended learning, identify the key benefits, explain the various blended learning models, and wrap up with reflection questions and next steps.

A Precise Definition of Blended Learning

The language we use to define an idea helps create clarity about what we are working toward. This is especially important for a term like blended learning. The sudden shift to distance and online learning in 2020 led to increased interest in blended learning. As a result, this term has been thrown around often, but it does not always have a clear definition. This has resulted in a degree of murkiness about the actual meaning. *Blended learning* is the combination of active, engaged learning online combined with active, engaged learning offline to provide students with more control over the time, place, pace, and path of their learning.

> *Blended learning* is the combination of active, engaged learning online combined with active, engaged learning offline to provide students with more control over the time, place, pace, and path of their learning.

My adaptation of researchers Heather Staker and Michael B. Horn's (2012) often-cited definition is rooted in constructivist principles emphasizing the student's role as an active agent in the learning process. I wanted the definition of blended learning to emphasize the importance of using offline and online learning to position the student at the center of the learning experience. The students must be the ones doing, making, thinking, discussing, questioning, problem solving, collaborating, and reflecting.

At its core, blended learning is a fundamental shift in control from the teacher to the learner. There are several blended learning models that give students different degrees of control over these four key elements of their experience: (1) time, (2) place, (3) pace, and (4) path. Students are not going to control all these aspects of their learning all the time. But teachers who use blended learning do aim to design and facilitate learning experiences that give students *more* control over their experience.

Blended learning offers an alternative to entirely face-to-face or entirely online classes, both of which have their disadvantages. Traditional instruction has been criticized for not giving learners agency, autonomy, or access to personalized learning opportunities, while online learning has been scrutinized for a lack of community and student interaction as well as lower levels of motivation and achievement, especially for marginalized groups (Mehta & Aguilera, 2020). Blended learning can help teachers maximize the opportunities for social learning and peer-to-peer interaction in the face-to-face learning environment while leveraging the affordances of an online learning environment. Students benefit from the opportunity to be part of a learning community while also directing their learning, exploring concepts at their own pace, and accessing learning customized for their specific needs and skills (Kundu, Bej, & Rice, 2021; Sahni, 2019; Shemshack & Spector, 2020).

The Purpose or Value of a Shift to Blended Learning

The messaging I have seen about the purpose and value of blended learning since 2020 seems to have been more reactive—a response to the pandemic—instead of proactive: an approach to educating students that is more likely to yield high-quality learning outcomes for *all* students. The *why*, or value, behind a shift to blended learning cannot be a reaction to a moment in time or a specific event. That isn't inspiring and is unlikely to result in long-term transformation. Instead, the why behind this shift in our approach to teaching and learning should be because it is better for teachers and students.

It is more likely to create engaging learning environments, in class and online, that honor learner variability and meet the diversity of student needs.

Teaching is a complex and multifaceted profession. The myriad demands on teachers' time and energy require that they have a clear why. If you ask teachers, "Why do you teach? What motivated you to do this challenging work? What do you value in your work?" they will often, in my experience, mention working with young people as a driving force or the desire to cultivate lifelong learners. In addition, when asked to describe a successful learning experience, teachers almost always include some form of the word *engage* in their answers: *engaging, engaged, engagement.* So, if our goal is to connect with young learners, cultivate a joy of learning in

> The *why*, or value, behind a shift to blended learning cannot be a reaction to a moment in time or a specific event. That isn't inspiring and is unlikely to result in long-term transformation. Instead, the why behind this shift in our approach to teaching and learning should be because it is better for teachers and students.

them, and actively engage them in student-centered learning, we should be designing and facilitating with those objectives in mind.

I am no different from the teachers I've worked with throughout my career. As I discussed in the introduction, the why driving my initial shift to blended learning was my desire to increase student engagement. What I want for your classroom is the same as what I wanted for my own classroom: I wanted students to *want* to be there—physically or virtually. I wanted them to be curious, participate in discussions, collaborate with peers, and feel comfortable taking risks.

Student engagement and teacher engagement are reciprocal. The more engaged students are, the more likely teachers are to be cognitively and emotionally engaged at work and satisfied with their work (Roth, Assor, Kanat-Maymon, & Kaplan, 2007; Tucker, 2020b). Teacher engagement and retaining quality educators should be everyone's concern. Because of the challenges of the COVID-19 pandemic, teachers are tired and feeling burned out (Pressley, 2021). They need a more rewarding and sustainable way to approach the profession. Leaders must support teachers in exploring alternative approaches to their work to ensure that both student engagement and teacher engagement remain high.

Key Benefits of Blended Learning

When I asked the teachers participating in my doctoral research study to define *blended learning* in their own words, their definitions provided insight into the aspects of blended learning they valued most, pictured in figure 1.1. They identified three key aspects of blended learning: (1) student agency, (2) differentiation, and (3) control over the pace of learning (Tucker, 2020b).

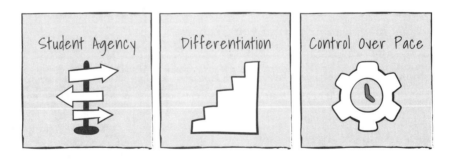

FIGURE 1.1: Three key benefits of blended learning.

These experienced blended learning teachers saw the dramatic impact that increased agency had on their students' motivation and desire to learn. They valued the time and space created by blended learning to effectively differentiate learning for small groups of students and individual learners with different needs, skills, language proficiencies, and interests. Finally, they recognized the students were more successful when they had more control over the pace at which they consumed and processed information and navigated tasks. Let's unpack all three.

Blended Learning Benefit 1: Student Agency

Student agency is learners' ability to make key decisions about their learning experience and can have a positive impact on their engagement over time (Jang, Kim, & Reeve, 2012; Patall et al., 2019). As students make decisions in a lesson, they have the power to pursue learning from an angle of interest, which is likely to make it more interesting and meaningful for them.

Agency comes from the Latin word *agentia*, which means *doing*. This doing requires that the learner take an active role in the learning process. A constructivist approach to blended learning strives to shift students to the center of learning, enabling them to construct meaning both through individual processes and interactions with the other members of the learning community.

There are three moments in a learning experience when we should consider giving students the agency to make decisions, as pictured in figure 1.2 (page 20). I represent them here as three questions: (1) What?, (2) How?, and (3) Why?

Student Agency Over the *What*

Students have unique interests and personal passions that a one-size-fits-all design cannot accommodate. Teachers can give students a degree of agency over the *what*, or the subject or topic. Perhaps students decide on the specific aspect of a larger topic they want to focus on or the lens they want to look through for an assignment or project.

For example, a high school English teacher might shift from requiring that all students research Elizabethan England to allowing small groups of students to select an aspect of that time period to focus on in their research. If the goal of the activity is to build their background knowledge via research to complement their reading of *Romeo and Juliet*, students do not all need to research the same thing to accomplish those objectives. Instead, groups could choose to research entertainment, gender roles, fashion, the plague and other illnesses, the monarchy, crime and punishment, or myriad other topics to learn about the Elizabethan era.

What?	Select the subject or topic.	• What do *students* want to focus on? • Is there an aspect of the larger topic they are particularly interested in? • Can they select the lens they look through for a particular assignment?
How?	Decide on the process or tools.	• How will they complete the task? • What steps will they take? • Which tools will they use? • How will they track their own progress toward completion?
Why?	Define the purpose and create a product.	• Why are they doing this work? • What is the purpose of a task, assignment, or project? • Given that purpose, what type of product do they want to create to demonstrate their learning? • How would they feel most successful sharing or expressing their learning?

FIGURE 1.2: Three opportunities for student agency.

Similarly, a third-grade teacher building an animal habitat playlist, or sequence of learning activities, can invite students to select the animal they would enjoy focusing on for this playlist. Giving students the freedom to choose the animal they focus on can transform an assignment into an experience that students are excited about and interested in.

Instead of asking all students to read the same text or focus on the same topic, how can we build student choice into our work and allow students to personalize their experience by aligning the work to their interests?

Student Agency Over the *How*

All learners have specific preferences about how they accomplish particular tasks: the process they work through and the tools they use. Some students enjoy working online using computer programs, and others enjoy a more tactile experience working with pencils, markers, and paper. The goal of giving students agency around how they accomplish a task is recognizing these different learning preferences and being flexible about how students complete an assignment or project. It is essential to make sure the objective is clear, offer support as students work, and allow them to decide *how* they want to work toward those objectives.

During the pandemic, many teachers worried about student access to resources and materials. Access and equity were important considerations during their design work. Teachers did not want to require students to complete tasks or projects that would be impossible given their access to resources and support. Prioritizing student choice and allowing students to decide how they wanted to complete a particular task or approach an assignment when working remotely was one way to ensure that all students could be successful.

For example, suppose teachers ask elementary students to practice number combinations. They could invite parents to print a review sheet or use items in their home environments (for example, buttons, coins, beans, pasta) to arrange in different combinations of numbers. Then they could document and share their learning via a picture of written work or a short video explaining the number combinations they created with their selected items. Alternatively, students who enjoy working on the computer could practice combining numbers using a mathematics program.

Whether or not they design a project to accommodate student preferences, teachers must be clear about what students should know or be able to do by the project's conclusion (DuFour, DuFour, Eaker, Many, & Mattos, 2016). To accomplish this, a teacher of a project-based secondary science class might employ a project proposal form, such as that pictured in figure 1.3 (page 22), to give students the agency to decide how they want to approach a particular project. The proposal form asks them to articulate the steps they would move through and the tools and resources they would use before beginning each project. Then the teacher can review each student's plan before they all start their projects. The teacher, in this scenario, uses her expertise to provide feedback and suggestions on the proposals, ensuring that they are well thought out and would likely lead students to accomplish the stated objectives.

Student Agency Over the *Why*

Understanding the purpose of an assignment, task, or project is the first step in appreciating the value of the work students are doing. Yet, articulating the *why* is easy to neglect as teachers race to cover the curriculum. It's critical that you have a clear why to drive your decision making and regularly challenge students to think about the value of the work they are doing.

If teachers are going to invite students to decide how they demonstrate or share their learning, students have to get comfortable thinking about why they are learning a particular concept or practicing a skill. Teachers might ask students to ponder the following questions.

Essential Project-Based Learning Design Elements	Questions to Consider	Your Proposed Plan
Challenging problem or question	What problem or question do you want to pursue and attempt to answer?	
Sustained inquiry	How will you attempt to learn about and understand this problem or question? What information would be helpful to collect?	
Authenticity	What is the context of your project? How is it grounded in the real world? What real-world processes, tasks, and tools will you use?	
Student voice and choice	What key decisions will you need to make as you move through this project?	
Reflection	How will you reflect on your learning as you move through this project? What reflection strategy would be most effective for you?	
Critique and revision	At what points during this project would feedback be most useful? Who would you like to gather feedback from during this project?	
Public product	How will you demonstrate what you learned? What product will you create?	

FIGURE 1.3: Project-based learning proposal form.

*Visit **go.SolutionTree.com/technology** for a free reproducible version of this figure.*

- Why is this concept important? How does this concept connect to other ideas they've learned? How does it extend their thinking on a topic or issue?

- What is the value of mastering a specific skill? How will they use this skill in their lives beyond the classroom? How will this specific skill help them to communicate, problem solve, or learn more effectively in the future?

Once students have considered these questions, they need to decide how to communicate or express what they learned. Students may feel more confident expressing what they know or can do in writing; others may be more at ease recording a video to explain what they learned. Still, others may want to draw, sketch, or create a concept map to surface their learning visually. One strategy for allowing students the agency to decide how they want to share their learning at the end of a learning cycle or unit is to provide a project choice board with a range of options for them to choose from, as pictured in figure 1.4.

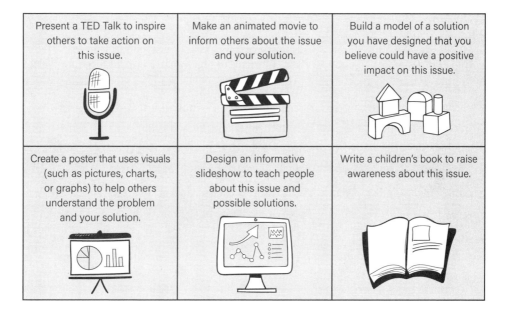

FIGURE 1.4: Project choice board example.

You may ask, "How do you grade the students' work if they all create something different?" Instead of grading the product (for example, specific aspects of a poster, model, or movie), we need to assess students' content knowledge and skills from the artifact they've created. If you use a rubric aligned to the standards or the learning objectives, then the specific product students produce to demonstrate their learning can be flexible. For example, imagine you are asking students to construct an argument as a culminating project. The goal is for students to take a position on an issue related to the curriculum, conduct online and offline research to gather evidence to support their positions, and communicate a compelling and cohesive argument. Their argument may take the form of a live debate with a classmate, an argumentative essay, a digital infographic, or a recorded speech. Even though students can communicate their position in a variety of ways, you can still use the same standards-aligned rubric to assess the clarity of the claims, quality and relevance of evidence, and effectiveness of the structure or organization of ideas.

Blended Learning Benefit 2: Differentiation and Personalization

Educators and others often use the terms *differentiation* and *personalization* interchangeably, but they are different. The most crucial distinction between the two is the person making the decisions about the learning. Differentiation is teacher focused, while personalization is learner focused (Bray & McClaskey, 2014).

Differentiation

Differentiation is the teacher moves we make to ensure that our design, instruction, and facilitation meet the spectrum of student needs in a class. Classes are composed of learners with various skills, needs, language proficiencies, funds of knowledge, prior experience, and interests. When teachers design differentiated learning experiences, they use formative assessment data to meet the needs of a diverse population of students. Differentiated instruction expert Carol Ann Tomlinson (2017) emphasizes that differentiation is a proactive approach to design. It is not simply about assigning more or less of something but rather ensuring that the task is appropriate for the specific learner or group of learners. It strives to meet students where they are in their learning journeys so everyone can be successful in making progress toward mastering the learning objectives.

For example, a second-grade teacher providing instruction focused on the reading strategy of asking and answering questions can begin by looking at the most recent reading assessment data to understand where each student is in terms of reading skills (fluency and comprehension). Using those data, she can select texts that are accessible for students at different reading levels and create scaffolds to support students as they practice the skill of asking and answering questions. She can write the words *who*, *what*, *where*, *when*, and *how* on the board or notecards for students to visually reference as they practice asking questions about the text. The teacher may guide the experience for a group that needs more support, reading the text together and stopping periodically to engage in the process of asking and answering the questions together. When working with higher-level readers, the teacher might read and model the reading strategy for the group, work through an example together, then release students to continue working in pairs or on their own.

In this example, the teacher uses data to understand the students' current reading abilities, groups them strategically, designs instruction and models to meet each group's needs, and provides the scaffolds and support necessary for every student to be successful. The teacher makes the decisions about the learning.

Personalization

Personalization is distinct from differentiation because it isn't simply the teacher making the decisions. The teacher and student work in concert to articulate learning goals, monitor progress toward those goals, select specific learning strategies, and co-construct learning experiences. As such, personalizing learning requires a partnership between the learner and the teacher.

Researchers Susan Patrick, Kathryn Kennedy, and Allison Powell (2013) provide a working definition stating that *personalization* is "tailoring learning for each student's strengths, needs and interests—including enabling student voice and choice in what, how, when, and where they learn—to provide flexibility and supports to ensure mastery of the highest standards possible" (p. 4). This language emphasizes the unique nature of each student and the need to design learning experiences that speak to individual needs and interests by prioritizing student agency and allowing students to make key decisions in the learning process. Teachers can't know what each student might enjoy or what might appeal to students' interests or learning preferences at any given moment, which is why they need to design with voice and choice in mind (Hastie, Rudisill, & Wadsworth, 2013). That makes it possible for *students* to decide how they want to approach a task or what aspect of a topic would be particularly interesting to them.

In addition to prioritizing student agency, teachers working with students to personalize learning need to carve out time to engage students in conversations about their needs, preferences, and progress. Conferencing is a cornerstone of personalization because it provides teachers and learners with consistent opportunities to check in, discuss learners' progress toward mastery, and adjust their path to ensure the learning experiences meet their specific needs. Ideally, you are trying to design learning experiences that are within each student's *zone of proximal development* (ZPD; Vygotsky, 1978)—the space between what students can do without support and what they can do with support from a teacher or their classmates. The goal is to challenge learners without presenting learning activities outside of their ZPD.

To effectively build agency into the design of the learning and to have the time and space to facilitate conferences, teachers will need to explore alternative instructional models. Personalized learning in a one-size-fits-all, teacher-led lesson in which the teacher must orchestrate all parts of the experience is impossible. It is important to note that blended learning does not

> It is important to note that blended learning does not equate to personalized learning, but it can provide a sustainable path toward personalization.

equate to personalized learning, but it can provide a sustainable path toward personalization.

Before teachers can design personalized learning experiences, it is helpful to keep key markers of personalized learning in mind. Figure 1.5 is informed by my teaching and coaching experience combined with the work of Patrick and colleagues (2013) for the Aurora Institute (formerly known as the International Association for K–12 Online Learning or iNACOL), along with creative learning strategist Barbara Bray and personalized learning expert Kathleen McClaskey (2014).

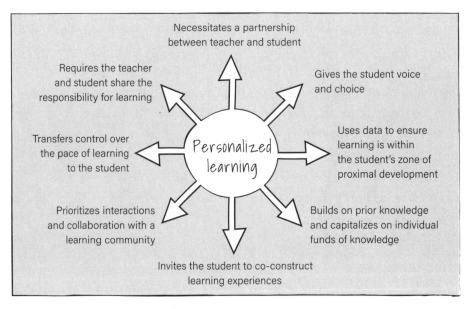

Source: Bray & McClaskey, 2014; Patrick et al., 2013.

FIGURE 1.5: Markers of personalized learning.

Moving toward personalized learning will be a work in progress. Instead of feeling daunted by the prospect of personalizing learning, we must see it as an ongoing journey. It is something we can work toward, and blended learning models will make it easier to achieve.

Blended Learning Benefit 3: Control Over Pace

Students consume and process information and navigate complex tasks at their own pace. Yet, traditional approaches to instruction do not allow students to dictate the pace of their learning. Instead, teachers usher students through learning activities on a fixed time line. Patrick and her colleagues (2013) make the point:

> Integrating technology and teaching allows students to fully master content and skills, and at the pace that's right for them . . . . Think about it this way: an average classroom sets a "speed limit" for the class—bounded by grade-level standards and assessments—making it hard for some students to catch up and holding others from moving ahead when they're ready. (p. 11)

The one-size-fits-all approach can lead to frustration, disillusionment, or boredom. When students feel rushed through content or learning activities, they do not feel valued. Whether consciously or unconsciously, they realize that the quality of *their* learning is not the priority. When students feel like the pace is too slow, they may disengage, become bored, and attempt to create their own diversions. Many of the disruptions and classroom management issues that arise in schools are the product of classes moving too quickly or too slowly for learners (McCallum, Schultz, Sellke, & Spartz, 2015; Postholm, 2013).

The strategic blend of active, engaged learning in class and online can allow teachers to let go of the lockstep approach that has characterized education for hundreds of years. Instead, they can design learning experiences that invite students to control the pace of their learning to ensure all students have the time and space to engage in deep and meaningful learning experiences.

Student agency, differentiation and personalization, and control over the pace, which are three key aspects of high-quality blended learning, are woven throughout this book. I highlight how blended learning makes it possible for educators to prioritize student agency, allowing them to make key decisions about their learning, effectively differentiate and even personalize learning, and leverage the various models to give students control over the pace of their learning. When we design and facilitate learning that prioritizes student agency, differentiates and allows students to personalize the experience, and shifts control over the pace of learning to the students, we are more likely to create learning experiences that meet their diverse needs and ensure *all* of them make progress toward mastering grade-level standards.

Blended Learning Models

Blended learning is an umbrella term. Underneath the umbrella are many different models, as illustrated in figure 1.6 (page 28), that give students different degrees of control over the time, place, pace, and path of their learning.

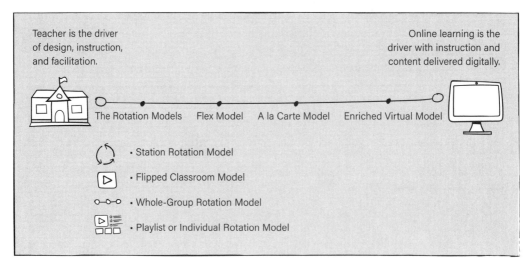

Source: Staker & Horn, 2012.

FIGURE 1.6: Taxonomy of blended learning models.

On one end of the spectrum are the rotation models, which position the teacher as the driver—actively designing, instructing, and facilitating learning. On the other end of the spectrum are the flex, a la carte, and enriched virtual models, which rely heavily on online learning to deliver content and instruction. These models often outsource much of the design work and instruction to digital programs or platforms that teachers may not have access to, so this book does not cover them extensively.

This book focuses primarily on the rotation models, which work beautifully in a classroom, online, or in a blend of the two. The rotation models rely on teachers' content-area and pedagogical expertise combined with their creativity to design dynamic learning experiences, provide instruction synchronously in small groups or asynchronously with video, and facilitate the learning by guiding students as they make progress toward learning objectives. In chapter 3 (page 47), we'll do a deep dive into the various rotation models and explore how teachers can use them to combine active engaged learning online and offline.

As we embark on this journey, I encourage you to visualize what you would like to see in your future classroom.

- What scenes do you hope to create?
- How is the room set up, and how are students using the space?
- What are you doing? How are you using your class time? Where are you investing your finite time and energy?
- What are your students doing? How are they driving the learning?

- What qualities and characteristics are your students exhibiting?
- What do your students' interactions look like? How are they engaging with each other?

Wrap-Up and Next Steps

The landscape of teaching and learning is shifting. This shift began with the influx of technology in classrooms, and the COVID-19 pandemic has only accelerated it. Instead of reacting to the unprecedented changes brought on by the pandemic, we must be proactive and use this reality as a catalyst for much-needed change in education.

Teachers need mindsets, skill sets, and toolsets that are nimble and allow them to confidently navigate flexible learning landscapes. Blended learning provides a path for teachers to effectively meet students where they are in terms of their skills, abilities, interests, language proficiencies, and exceptionalities. By strategically weaving together active, engaged learning online with active, engaging learning offline, teachers can give students more agency over their learning, differentiate and personalize learning experiences, and shift control over the pace of learning from teacher to student. The rest of this book is dedicated to helping educators explore sustainable ways to design, instruct, and facilitate learning that shifts students to the center of learning where they belong.

Consider taking the following next steps as a way to further what you've learned. See also the reflection questions on page 30.

- Student agency is a key aspect of blended learning. Use what you have learned in this chapter to revisit a lesson, learning experience, or assessment you have used with your students in the past, and ponder the following questions.
    - ¤ How can you build student agency, or meaningful choice, into this experience for your students?
    - ¤ Will they get to decide what lens they look through, how they complete the assignment or what materials they use, or the product they create to demonstrate their learning?
- Modify your existing lesson, learning experience, or assessment to include at least one element of student agency. Share what you have created with your collaborative team on your campus or online for feedback.

Chapter 1: The Basics of Blended Learning— Reflect and Discuss

I encourage you to pause here to reflect on or discuss the following questions. If you are reading this book on your own, you can reflect on these questions in a blog post, publish your thoughts on your favorite social media platform, or capture your thoughts in a journal or notebook. If you are reading this book as part of a book club or book study, use the following questions to facilitate vibrant in-person or online discussions.

1. How might the ways in which students consume media and interact with the world beyond the classroom impact their expectations of and feelings about school?

2. When you read the definition of blended learning provided at the beginning of this chapter, did it align with your prior knowledge about blended learning? What stood out to you about this definition compared to what you've heard about blended learning in the past?

3. How are you currently blending online and offline learning?

4. How do you incorporate voice and choice into the design of your lessons? Based on your work with students, what is the potentially positive impact of giving students agency?

5. If you had to describe the difference between differentiation and personalization to a colleague or friend, what would you say?

6. Do you currently differentiate or personalize learning? What does that look like in your class? What is challenging about differentiating or personalizing learning?

7. When do students get to control the pace of their learning in your class? How can you build more opportunities for students to control the pace of their learning?

CHAPTER 2
YOUR BLENDED LEARNING TECHNOLOGY TOOLBOX

No one tool can solve every problem. The Swiss army knife does a valiant job of trying, but there are still various jobs that cannot be completed with a corkscrew, toothpick, tiny spoon, or a series of miniature knives. To get things done in your daily life, you're likely to need a greater variety of tools. Similarly, a complex and multifaceted profession like teaching requires a robust toolbox. That does not mean that we as teachers need a ton of technology tools to embrace blended learning, but it does demand thoughtful consideration of what we are trying to accomplish in classrooms and which tools help us reach those objectives or outcomes.

A teacher transitioning to blended learning will need a toolbox that includes technology tools, like a learning management system (LMS)—which functionas as the students' online classroom—and a collaborative work suite, like Google or Microsoft, that makes producing, sharing, and revising work online more manageable. In addition to these literal tools, blended learning teachers need metaphorical tools, or ways of thinking about learning, like the four Cs of 21st century learning. As teachers design blended learning experiences, they can use the four Cs as a lens to ensure that they are prioritizing critical thinking, communication, collaboration, and creativity. They can also use the SAMR framework to guide their thinking about the role of technology in a lesson. This combination of physical, digital, and mental tools is critical to cultivating a dynamic, engaging, and student-centered blended learning environment.

The most important idea I want you to take away from this chapter is that it isn't how many tools you use but rather *how* you use the tools you have.

In this chapter, I discuss the purpose of an LMS in a blended learning environment. I encourage you to select technology tools that allow you to prioritize the four Cs of 21st century learning in your design work, and explore four key questions to consider when using technology. Finally, I'll review the SAMR framework and encourage you to use it to guide a thoughtful self-assessment of the role that technology is playing in your lessons. The more intentionality you bring to building your literal and metaphorical toolbox, the more confident you will feel as you design lessons using the various blended learning models.

> It isn't how many tools you use but rather *how* you use the tools you have.

Your Learning Management System as Online Classroom

Since blended learning combines active, engaged learning in class with active, engaged learning online, teachers need an online space where students can access information, resources, and each other. Essentially, you need an online classroom to complement your physical classroom. An LMS provides you and your students with a virtual hub as they work online.

Schools and district leaders typically select the LMS for teachers and students, purchasing a schoolwide or districtwide license. A panel of teachers may have the opportunity to voice preferences in this selection process, and help identify desirable LMS features (for example, assessment, discussion, and audio feedback functionality), but they rarely have the power to make these decisions. District leaders will likely select an LMS that integrates well with their existing grade-reporting system or collaborative work suite.

Just like you spend a day or two before the school year starts setting up your physical classroom in preparation to welcome students back to school, you will need to spend time setting up your LMS. Use the checklist in figure 2.1 to guide this setup process.

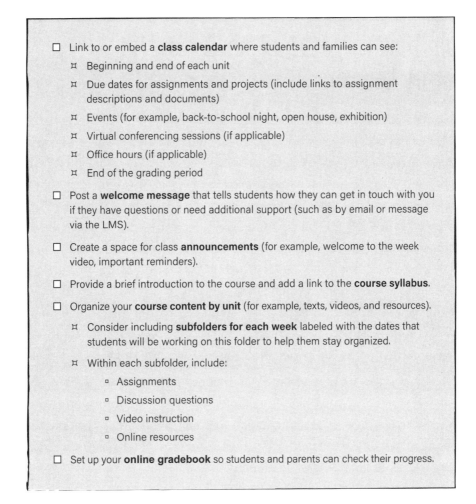

□ Link to or embed a **class calendar** where students and families can see:

  ¤ Beginning and end of each unit

  ¤ Due dates for assignments and projects (include links to assignment descriptions and documents)

  ¤ Events (for example, back-to-school night, open house, exhibition)

  ¤ Virtual conferencing sessions (if applicable)

  ¤ Office hours (if applicable)

  ¤ End of the grading period

□ Post a **welcome message** that tells students how they can get in touch with you if they have questions or need additional support (such as by email or message via the LMS).

□ Create a space for class **announcements** (for example, welcome to the week video, important reminders).

□ Provide a brief introduction to the course and add a link to the **course syllabus**.

□ Organize your **course content by unit** (for example, texts, videos, and resources).

  ¤ Consider including **subfolders for each week** labeled with the dates that students will be working on this folder to help them stay organized.

  ¤ Within each subfolder, include:

    □ Assignments

    □ Discussion questions

    □ Video instruction

    □ Online resources

□ Set up your **online gradebook** so students and parents can check their progress.

FIGURE 2.1: Checklist—Setting up your virtual classroom.

*Visit **go.SolutionTree.com/technology** for a free reproducible version of this figure.*

If you set up your LMS in advance of the first day of school, then you can ask students to complete a scavenger hunt activity challenging them to explore their online classroom. They can do this synchronously in class with peers or asynchronously for homework to familiarize themselves with their LMS. It is important to check in with students about their access to a device and internet connection at home before assigning asynchronous online work for them to complete outside of class. The goal is to get them comfortable visiting your LMS daily to check assignments and access resources.

Tools That Target the Four Cs of 21st Century Learning

Too often, technology isolates learners instead of connecting them. There is a place for video lessons and online review or practice. But if those are the only ways teachers use technology, students are likely to become disillusioned with the online learning component of their blended learning experience. Instead, if you design your online learning using the lens of the four Cs of 21st century learning (Partnership for 21st Century Learning, 2019), you are more likely to create learning experiences that students will enjoy because they are cognitively challenging and socially engaging (Gebre, Saroyan, & Bracewell, 2014). The four Cs are critical skills students need to fully participate in an increasingly interconnected and global community, where they will need to think critically to understand complex problems, communicate their ideas in person and online, collaborate with diverse groups of people, and be creative in their approach to solving problems and accomplishing a range of tasks.

Table 2.1 provides a brief definition of each of the four Cs and a few examples of what these activities look like in practice. As you design your online learning activities, whether they are part of a station rotation, whole-group rotation, flipped classroom, or playlist, strive to prioritize at least one of the four Cs in your design to keep student interest and engagement high.

Four Key Questions to Consider When Using Technology

In a conversation on my podcast, *The Balance* (Tucker, 2021b), personalized learning expert Paul France encourages teachers to consider four questions when designing learning experiences that use technology.

1. Is the technology minimizing complexity?
2. Does technology maximize individual power and potential?
3. Does technology reimagine learning?
4. Is technology preserving or enhancing human connection?

Table 2.1: Four Cs of 21st Century Learning

The Four Cs	Description	In Action
Critical Thinking	Analyze, synthesize, evaluate, and interpret to creatively solve problems, develop an argument, demonstrate understanding, or reach a conclusion.	**Tell me how challenge:** Ask students to verbally surface their thinking by talking you through the process they used to solve a problem or approach a task. Analyze a text, video, or podcast to reach conclusions or craft a strong claim. Conduct research (individually and collaboratively), and synthesize information from multiple sources to reach conclusions.
Communication	Engage speaking and listening skills to take part in academic discourse or communicate with peers to unpack key concepts and effectively navigate shared tasks.	Participate in a range of online academic discussions: unpack complex texts, topics, issues, videos, podcasts, and so on with a community of peers. • Real time in virtual breakout rooms • Asynchronous, text based • Asynchronous, video based
Collaboration	Collaborate with peers on shared tasks and challenges in shared digital spaces online.	Explore teacher-curated resources. Build background with online exploration. Work with peers to construct artifacts of learning, such as multimedia presentations, time lines, graphics, or digital posters.
Creativity	Think outside of the box, and apply learning in creative ways that appeal to learners.	Encourage students to use online creation tools to produce artifacts of their learning. • Original podcasts • Digital stories • 3-D models • Graphics and infographics

Source: Adapted from Partnership for 21st Century Learning, 2019.

These questions can function to frame and focus your use of technology to ensure that it is necessary, enhances the quality of the learning experience, and functions to strengthen the learning community.

Is the Technology Minimizing Complexity?

Technology should make a task easier to complete, not harder. France makes the point that we all carry our phones everywhere because they help us navigate everyday tasks more effectively and efficiently (as cited in Tucker, 2021b). They tell us the time, provide reminders and calendar alerts, help us navigate toward new locations, and connect us with the people we love. The same should be true for technology in education. It should help learners by removing potential barriers that might make a task more challenging to complete or an objective harder to meet. For example, students who struggle to type can use features like voice-to-text in digital documents to save time and communicate more effectively. If the technology is not minimizing complexity, then it is likely a superficial add-on that may make the task more cumbersome for students.

Does Technology Maximize Individual Power and Potential?

Technology can be used to shift traditional power structures in classrooms to move students to the center of learning. When you use technology to maximize individual power and potential, you allow students to drive their learning by making meaningful choices and pursuing learning through a lens of interest. Instead of making all students read a particular text to practice a specific skill, like predicting or summarizing, the wealth of online texts makes it possible to offer students meaningful choices, allowing them to select a text of interest. Similarly, technology tools offer students opportunities to use devices to capture photos, videos, and audio to document their learning instead of relying exclusively on written descriptions and definitions. The beauty of being connected to so much information and so many digital tools and platforms online is that students can and should enjoy more agency or power when deciding what they learn and how they learn. In addition, they can reach their full potential when they decide what they want to create to demonstrate that learning.

Does Technology Reimagine Learning?

Innovative teaching and learning consultant George Couros (Tucker, 2021a) defines *innovation* simply as "better ways of teaching and learning." Technology can be a catalyst for exciting change in our approach to teaching and learning. Before technology became widespread in classrooms, you may have felt unable to provide students with the flexibility to engage with information in various formats, pursue passion projects, or create authentic artifacts of their learning. However, technology opens the door for us to reimagine the way we have traditionally designed learning experiences to ask, "Is there a better way to do this?" For example, instead of asking students to write a report or research paper on a topic they have investigated, teachers can offer them the opportunity to create a digital artifact, like an infographic or multimedia informational website, to demonstrate their learning.

Is Technology Preserving or Enhancing Human Connection?

Technology can prove isolating when students are only asked to consume media or practice and review with adaptive software or online programs. There isn't anything inherently wrong with using technology this way, but it should not be the *only* way we use it. Technology can strengthen the learning community by allowing for more equitable conversations and encouraging collaboration around shared tasks. We must strive to use technology to strengthen relationships and enhance connections among students. For example, instead of relying soley on whole-group discussions, which may present barriers for students who are shy, need more time to process, or struggle with social anxiety, online discussions give learners more control over the experience and provide every student an opportunity to participate in the class dialogue. This can make discussions more inclusive and equitable, while also helping students get to know one another because everyone is contributing to the conversation.

Technology and the SAMR Framework

Just as asking students to complete a self-assessment of their work helps them develop their metacognitive muscles and become more aware of their areas of strength and weakness, you can approach your technology use with the same critical eye (Baas, Castelijns, Vermeulen, Martens, & Segers, 2015; Braund & DeLuca; 2018). Each person has a different level of comfort and proficiency with technology. As a result, the shift to blended learning may push you outside of your comfort zone when designing learning experiences that use technology. You may not feel confident leveraging the power of technology *yet*, but you will eventually develop higher levels of self-efficacy if you are patient with yourself and committed to learning. If you begin your design work with the four questions presented in the previous section and regularly conduct self-assessments of your lessons using the SAMR framework (Puentedura, 2013), you will develop a more complete understanding of how you are using technology and where you have room to grow.

The SAMR framework, shown in figure 2.2 (page 40), is a four-tier approach to thinking about the role of technology in a lesson (Puentedura, 2013; Terada, 2020).

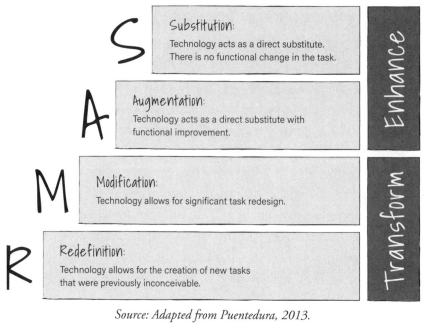

Source: Adapted from Puentedura, 2013.

FIGURE 2.2: SAMR framework.

Let's explore the four levels and how you might progress through them.

Substitution

Substitution is the first tier of this framework and the place most people begin when using technology. At this level, technology is simply substituting for a task that can be done offline. You might ask students to complete a digital worksheet, answer questions via a digital form, or complete a quiz online instead of on paper. Or it might look like asking students to read an article online instead of printing it out. The technology in these examples does not change the task. Students are still completing the worksheet, taking the quiz, or reading the article even though it is happening online instead of offline.

Augmentation

Augmentation is the second tier of the SAMR framework. At this level, the technology is still substituting for a task that can be done offline, but there is some functional improvement that results from the technology. If you ask students to type a paper on Google Docs (https://docs.google.com) instead of writing on paper, students who struggle with the fine motor skills necessary to write or type can use the voice-to-text feature. Similarly, providing texts digitally makes it possible for students to manipulate the content, making it bigger or smaller in size. Digital books are increasingly equipped with accessibility features that make it easier for readers who have disabilities, like dyslexia, to access texts. You may also have the ability to provide different versions of the same article written at different Lexile levels to differentiate the experience and ensure the text is accessible for students at different reading levels.

Modification

Modification is the third tier of the SAMR framework and marks the shifts from technology for enhancing learning to technology for transformation, where the technology transforms or redefines the learning task. At this level, the technology is modifying the task, allowing for a significant redesign. For example, instead of asking students to label a map on paper, you can let students use Google Earth (https://earth.google.com) to create customized maps and drop pins in various locations, adding text, media, and links to their maps to track the development of a conflict or social movement. Then they can share the links to their maps with peers for feedback. As part of that feedback process, you can also explore using an asynchronous, video-based online discussion platform to facilitate discourse or peer feedback sessions that allow all students to participate in the conversation or activity. Video-based discussion can happen in a classroom as part of a station rotation or playlist, or it can happen asynchronously from home. Video-based dsicussions using a platform like Flipgrid (https://info.flipgride.com) give students the ability to re-record if they are not satisfied with their recording. It also allows students to self-pace through each other's explanations, leaving text or video comments for one another.

Redefinition

Redefinition is the fourth tier of the SAMR framework and marks the stage of technology use when a completely new task is possible because of technology. For example, students can produce and publish an original podcast, digital story, or website for an authentic audience and receive feedback on their work. You can have students go on virtual field trips, or connect them with experts or other classrooms around the world. At this stage, the technology should inspire you to think big about what students create, who they share their work with, and how they receive feedback on that work. This level of SAMR can make learning feel relevant and dynamic in a way that is hard to achieve when learning is confined to the walls of a physical classroom.

Progression Through the Levels

It's important to note that even though the SAMR framework depicts four levels with the implication that you should progress from substitution to redefinition, you will likely hit each of these stages of technology use at various times in your work with students. Sometimes you will use technology to substitute, like having students type a response and submit it digitally because it makes your life a bit easier in terms of workflow. Other times you'll dabble in redefinition to reimagine a task or assignment, allowing students to do something that may not have been possible before technology, like producing and publishing an original podcast.

Your technology use may not be linear in terms of progressing through the four levels of SAMR. Once you have experimented with redefinition, it doesn't mean that is all you will ever do. Instead, the goal is to be aware of how you are using technology to enhance and improve your experience teaching and your students' experience learning. That higher level of intentionality will translate into more meaningful technology integration as you weave together online and offline learning.

Wrap-Up and Next Steps

Your technology toolbox is a vital consideration as you transition to blended learning; it isn't so much the number of tools but rather how you are using them that counts. Setting up your LMS to establish a central location online where students can access everything they need for the online learning portions of a lesson alleviates confusion and frustration as they navigate online tasks. Ideally, you want to organize your LMS to provide students with everything they need to successfully navigate online learning with confidence and ease.

As you add additional tools and online platforms to your toolset, keep the four Cs in mind and design online learning experiences using them as a lens. The more you prioritize critical thinking, communication, collaboration, and creativity in your lessons, the more likely students are to find those tasks engaging. As you develop your confidence with technology, use the SAMR framework as a guide to think intentionally about how you are using the tools at your disposal. Nudge yourself to continually stretch and push your usage to include more advanced tiers of use, like augmentation and redefinition.

Along with the reflection questions on page 44, consider taking this next step to further what you have learned so far: think about an upcoming topic your students will learn about. For elementary students, it might be animals and their habitats, a holiday, a type of writing, a mathematical concept, or a season of the year. For secondary students, it might be learning about a country in Africa, a scientific phenomenon, a literary or art movement, or a famous person. To demonstrate their learning, students must create a presentation or an artifact that reflects what they know and can do. On your own or with a group of colleagues, think about what the product or presentation might look like at each level. Fill in the template in figure 2.3 by describing what the artifact might look like at each level of the SAMR framework.

Substitution: Technology acts as a direct substitute. There is no functional change in the task.	
Augmentation: Technology acts as a direct substitute with functional improvement.	
Modification: Technology allows for significant task redesign.	
Redefinition: Technology allows for the creation of new tasks that were previously inconceivable.	

FIGURE 2.3: Activity—Thinking through SAMR.

*Visit **go.SolutionTree.com/technology** for a free reproducible version of this figure.*

Chapter 2: Your Blended Learning Technology Toolbox—Reflect and Discuss

I encourage you to pause here to reflect on or discuss the following questions. If you are reading this book on your own, you can reflect on these questions in a blog post, publish your thoughts on your favorite social media platform, or capture your thoughts in a journal or notebook. If you are reading this book as part of a book club or book study, use the following questions to facilitate vibrant in-person or online discussions.

1. What is your reaction to thinking about your LMS as your online classroom? If you currently use an LMS, what features have been particularly helpful or useful? Have you organized your LMS in the ways the checklist provided in this chapter suggests? Are there items you would add to your personal checklist to ensure your LMS is as user friendly as possible for you, your students, and their parents?

2. When you design online learning experiences, what are students typically doing online? Would you categorize these activities as individual, collaborative, or a mix of the two? Which of the four Cs do you think you do the best job of prioritizing in your design work? Which of the four Cs would you like to spend more time and energy pulling into your design work? Brainstorm technology tools and activities you could use to get students thinking critically, communicating, collaborating, and creating online.

3. Which of the four questions presented by Paul France (Tucker, 2021b) resonates with you the most? Which area—minimizing complexity, maximizing individual power and potential, reimagining learning, or enhancing human connection—is the one you need to focus on the most as you blend online learning into your lessons? How might considering these questions during your design work impact the way you use technology?

4. Think about the four stages of the SAMR framework. Which tier do you currently spend the most time in? What types of activities or instructional strategies do you frequently use that fall into this tier? How might using this framework as a guide to engaging in a regular practice of self-assessment push you to continue growing? What resources do you have at your disposal if you get stuck on a particular tier?

Reference

Tucker, C. R. (2021b). Reclaiming personalized learning with Paul France [Podcast]. *The Balance.* Accessed at https://podcasts.apple.com/us/podcast /reclaiming-personalized -learning-with-paul-france/id1485751335 ?i=1000534012808 on November 24, 2021.

TEACHERS AS DESIGNERS OF LEARNING EXPERIENCES

After my home burned in the Tubbs Fire that devastated Santa Rosa, California, in 2017, I had my first interaction with an architect. Instead of rebuilding my home exactly as it had been before the fire, I decided to start from scratch and build my dream home. The architect asked me countless questions about how I used the space in my home, what my daily routine was like, what I had enjoyed about the home I lost, and what I would change. He listened attentively to my answers. He wanted to know me and to understand what I valued and enjoyed in a home. From these conversations, he produced an architectural plan and drawings of the house he envisioned for me. It was perfect! It incorporated every preference I had expressed and every request I had made. He personalized the design of my home based on our conversations and his understanding of me as an individual.

Once the blueprint was finalized, contractors and subcontractors did the actual work of building the structure. Over the course of a year and a half, they brought the architectural plan to life. As I move around my home enjoying the customized space, I'm so grateful to have found an architect who took the time to understand me: my needs, my interests, and my preferences.

Just like my architect took time to get to know me, as designers of learning experiences, we must do the same for our students. The following questions offer some ways to start.

- Who are they?
- What do they enjoy?
- What are they interested in?

- What are their learning preferences, needs, skills, abilities, language proficiencies, and so on?

- Do they like to work alone, with a partner, or as part of a group?

- How can we design learning experiences that meet them where they are in their learning journeys?

Our design work should strive to place learners, not teachers, at the center of learning. The students should do the thinking and the work in a classroom. My architect did not pick up a hammer or install insulation. His job was to design the home, not to build it. He combined a high-level understanding of construction and aesthetics to create a home to meet my specific needs. Similarly, educators must design dynamic learning experiences that strive to remove barriers and invite students to do the building and make meaning. It is *not* our job to do the work of constructing knowledge. That job belongs to the students.

> Educators must design dynamic learning experiences that strive to remove barriers and invite students to do the "building" and make meaning. It is *not* our job to do the work of constructing knowledge. That job belongs to the students.

When students grapple with new ideas, engage in conversations, collaborate around shared tasks, explore complex issues, and ask questions, that's how they learn. We must position students to be active, engaged participants in the learning process, regardless of whether that is happening in class, online, or a blend of the two learning landscapes. We should strive to design learning experiences that require the students to do the thinking *and* the work in a classroom. That demands new approaches to designing learning experiences.

In this chapter, I will discuss the taxonomy of blended learning models that range from the rotation models, which rely heavily on the teacher as designer, instructor, and facilitator, to the models that rely heavily on online learning as the backbone of the course. These models—flex, a la carte, and enriched virtual—require that schools invest significantly in online curriculum, and they often depart from the typical 8:00 a.m. to 3:00 p.m. school day. Because the majority of schools are still using a traditional bell schedule and may not have the financial resources to pay for a complete online curriculum, this book will focus on the rotation models, which are the most accessible of the blended learning models.

Blended Learning Models

It's impossible to meet the diverse needs in a class composed of thirty students if we only have one tool or instructional model for structuring a lesson. Yet many teachers still rely heavily, or even exclusively, on a whole-group, teacher-led approach to lesson design, which positions the teacher as the expert at the front of the room orchestrating the lesson and relegates the students to the role of receivers and passive consumers. Instead, teachers must strive to match the best instructional model to the specific objectives of a learning experience. You may feel reluctant to experiment with different models because they are new and unfamiliar. That's understandable. Trying anything new that is outside of your comfort zone or requires a risk may feel daunting and scary. But once you've learned how to use each model, you will become proficient at selecting the best one to meet learning goals and student needs.

How do you know what the "best" blended learning model is for a particular outcome? First, you must develop confidence in your ability to identify student learning goals and individual needs. It does not make sense to use the same instructional model for every objective or group of students. One model will not work for every situation, learning objective, or group of students.

Then comes understanding the different rotation models that fall under the umbrella of blended learning. What are they? How do they work? What do they look like in action? What is the teacher's role in each model? How does the model allow for student agency, differentiation or personalization, and control over the pace of learning?

Each model has its unique advantages. You may want to begin with a single model. Get to know the model, experiment with it, hit bumps, and adjust. After you have played with a single model and developed confidence with it, then you can build on your practice and select another blended learning model to experiment with. Remember, the transition to blended learning is a journey that takes time. Don't feel you need to master every model in your first year. It may take a few years before you feel confident matching the model with the objectives of a lesson or the specific needs of a group of learners, but it will happen.

Following are some questions to consider as you identify the model you want to use as you begin your blended learning journey. You can begin by considering logistical questions, like the number of deveices available in the classroom, which will impact the models you can use. If devices are limited, you will want to use the station rotation model, which does not require that all students be online simultaneously. Then you should consider what your role and focus in the lesson will be. Will you want to provide differentiated instruction, give students feedback, or facilitate individual conferences? Depending on your focus, you can select the model that will free you to engage in that work while allowing students opportunities to control their learning experience.

- How many devices do you have in your classroom? Do you have enough devices for each student? Will you have to be strategic about who uses devices and when?

- How do you want to use your time with students? Would you like to work with the whole group, small groups, or individual students? Do you plan to provide instruction, model a strategy or process, give real-time feedback, or guide practice and application?

- What do you want students to do during this lesson? Would that work be most successful if students worked alone, with a partner, or in a small group? Do you plan to pair or group them strategically, or would you prefer to allow them the flexibility to choose what they think will work best for them?

- Which elements of their learning—time, place, pace, and path— would be most beneficial for students to control during this lesson or learning experience?

The answers to these questions will help you identify the blended learning model or models you think will work best for you and your students. In the following sections, we'll review the four main blended learning rotation models: (1) station rotation, (2) whole-group rotation, (3) flipped classroom, and (4) playlist or individual rotation.

The Station Rotation Model

The *station rotation model* is composed of a series of learning activities that students rotate through. A typical station rotation has three types of stations: (1) teacher-led station, (2) online station, and (3) offline station. However, the total number of stations varies depending on a few factors. You may want to limit the number of students at a station to six or eight students, depending on the size of the class, which will determine the total number of stations. Similarly, the length of the class period may impact how many stations you design. For example, if you have a ninety-minute block period, you may choose to design a four-station rotation and have students spend twenty minutes at each station, completing the rotation in a single class. If you only have a forty-five or fifty-minute class period, you might decide to run four stations over two days, asking students to visit two stations each day for twenty minutes.

You may think of a station as a physical location in a classroom; however, a *station* is simply a learning activity. When you think about a station as a learning activity, it becomes easier to imagine using this model in class or entirely online. During the pandemic, many teachers visited my blog and social media to share their successes with designing virtual station rotations that used breakout rooms and included some offline asynchronous activities. Despite being entirely online, teachers were freed to meet with small groups of learners for their teacher-led station, facilitate conversation and collaboration among groups in breakout rooms, and allow self-paced learning with the asynchronous offline learning activities. The breakout-room feature offered in Zoom and a variety of other video-conferencing platforms makes it possible to facilitate small-group discussions and collaborative group work online to keep virtual classes feeling interactive and dynamic. If you're not familiar with the breakout-room feature of online conferencing tools like Zoom, now is the time to explore it.

When Should You Use the Station Rotation Model?

You may want to consider the station rotation model if any of the following apply to you.

- **You are frustrated by large class sizes:** The station rotation model makes it possible to create smaller learning communities within the larger class. If you feel that your classes are composed of too many students, you can use the station rotation model to break students into groups to allow for more interaction among members of the class.

- **You want to work directly with small groups of students:** The station rotation model provides you with dedicated time in the lesson to work with small groups of students to differentiate effectively and consistently. This small-group dynamic makes it possible for you to connect with every student during the lesson, responding to specific needs.

- **You plan to differentiate instruction:** You want to be able to model strategies, provide scaffolds, and adjust the level of academic rigor and complexity of the tasks you are asking students to complete. With the station rotation model, you can use formative assessment data or diagnostic data to group students strategically and differentiate models, supports, and scaffolds, as well as the level of academic rigor in the practice and application you are asking students to do at the various stations.

- **You want to encourage communication and collaboration among students:** The station rotation model positions groups of learners to work together to navigate tasks, engage in conversation, and provide peer support.

What Does the Station Rotation Model Look Like in Action?

A station rotation lesson requires that learners complete a series of learning activities, as pictured in figure 3.1. You can arrange furniture to support a variety of learning activities. For example, it may be helpful to arrange the teacher-led station at the front of the room so that you have access to a board to project information or media and also a view of the rest of the room. Just like at the theater, where actors are trained never to turn their backs to the audience, the same rule is true in a classroom. You should position yourself so you can quickly scan the room to see your students at work.

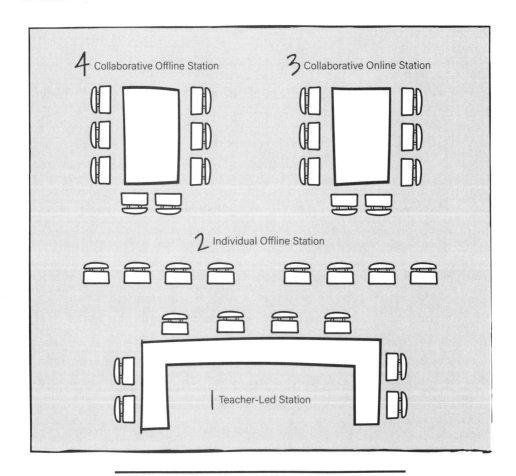

FIGURE 3.1: The station rotation lesson in action.

If the task is an individual one, it is better not to arrange students in a group formation since that implies collaboration. Instead, position them at individual desks to focus on the task at hand. Conversely, collaborative tasks require close physical proximity, so you will want to push desks together to facilitate that work. Ultimately, it is helpful if the furniture arrangement in a classroom reinforces the objective of each learning activity.

Let's take a look at an elementary and a secondary example of a station rotation (see figure 3.2).

Elementary Station Rotation	Reading or English Language Arts
Teacher-led station	The teacher groups students in mixed skill-level groups and uses the I do, we do, groups do, you do progression to support students in applying the reading strategy of asking and answering questions about a text using who, what, where, when, and why.
Online station	Individual students work with a reading program, like Lexia (www .lexialearning.com), that personalizes their reading practice based on their performance.
Offline station	Students work in pairs to practice a grammar concept that has already been introduced or review vocabulary using a graphic organizer or Frayer model (Frayer, Frederick, & Klausmeier, 1969) handout.

Secondary Station Rotation	Mathematics
Teacher-led station	The teacher groups students in skill-level groups and differentiates instruction based on the needs of each group to help members learn the steps to solving quadradic equations.
Online station	Students use the online graphing calcuator Desmos (www.desmos .com) to practice graphing different types of equations to spiral back to previously introduced concepts.
Offline station	Students work in collaborative groups to solve a real-world mathematics problem, applying what they are learning to a high-interest scenario.

FIGURE 3.2: Two examples of station rotation lessons.

There are various ways you can use the different types of stations to engage learners. However, it's common for teachers to get comfortable using stations in a particular way. For example, some teachers use their teacher-led stations exclusively to provide direct instruction. At the online station, students work with an online program or digital curriculum. The offline station is limited to worksheets or pencil-and-paper practice. Although there is nothing inherently wrong with using these strategies, students are unlikely to get excited about a station rotation lesson if that is all they can expect from their experience. If you mix up the types of learning activities you ask students to engage with at each station, they are more likely to enjoy the experience. Table 3.1 offers some ideas for using all three types of stations.

Table 3.1: Ideas for Designing Stations in a Station Rotation Lesson

Type of Station	Ideas for Use
Teacher-Led Station	• Differentiated instruction and support • I do, we do, groups do, you do (see page 88) • Guided practice and application • Real-time feedback on work in progress • Teacher-facilitated discussion or fishbowl (see page 109) • Host a question-and-answer session about a text, topic, or assignment

Online Station	• Personalized practice with adaptive software or an online program
	• Building background with online research and exploration
	• Multimedia lessons with:
	  ¤ Texts
	  ¤ Videos
	  ¤ Student-friendly podcasts
	  ¤ Interactive websites
	• Virtual field trips
	• Online scavenger hunts
	• Asynchronous online discussions:
	  ¤ Video-based
	  ¤ Text-based
	• Review games
	• Creating online artifacts of learning

Offline Station	• Makerspace activities (tinker and build)
	• Pencil-and-paper practice and review
	• Read and take notes
	• Writing tasks
	• Observe and document (write or draw)
	• Interview a classmate
	• Discussion:
	  ¤ Teacher-facilitated fishbowl
	  ¤ Four-corner conversations (see page 111)
	• Experiments
	• Science, technology, engineering, and mathematics challenges
	• Art projects

You can use the templates in figure 3.3 and figure 3.4 (page 56) to plan an in-class station rotation or to design a virtual station rotation. Remember that the number of stations can vary, so feel free to modify and adapt the templates as needed.

Target standard or standards:	
Learning objectives:	
Time in each station:	
Cue to move (for example, music, timer, lights, and so on):	
Technology needed:	
Next steps or may-do list:	
Station 1: Teacher-led Objective or skill: Description:	Station 2: Online Objective or skill: Description:
Station 3: Offline Objective or skill: Description:	Station 4: Your choice Objective or skill: Description:

FIGURE 3.3: Station rotation template for in-class lesson.

*Visit **go.SolutionTree.com/technology** for a free reproducible version of this figure.*

How Can You Ensure a Station Rotation Lesson Runs Smoothly?

The following pointers will help your first attempts at designing and implementing a station rotation run more smoothly.

- Use your teacher-led station for a range of activities beyond direct instruction: instruction, modeling, feedback, and discussion. The more you allow students to interact with ideas and each other in this station, the more informal formative assessment data you will collect by listening and observing.

- Use flexible groupings and match your grouping strategy to the objectives of the stations. You may want to consider the following grouping strategies.

Stations	Instructions			
Teacher-led station	Please attend the virtual conferencing session that your group has been assigned.			
		Names	Day and time	Video link
	Group 1			
	Group 2			
	Group 3			
	Objective: Directions:			
Online station	Objective: Directions:			
Offline station	Objective: Directions: Please post documentation of your work to:			

FIGURE 3.4: Virtual station rotation lesson template.

*Visit **go.SolutionTree.com/technology** for a free reproducible version of this figure.*

- **Mixed skill-level groups:** Provide peer support.

- **Skill-level groups:** Make it easier to differentiate instruction, scaffolds, and level of the academic rigor of tasks to ensure they are appropriate for each group.

- **Needs-based groups**: Rely on data to group students based on their specific needs.

- **Mixed-personality groups:** Strive to create groups composed of a mix of personalities that are more likely to navigate collaborative tasks in a productive way.

- **Mixed speaking and listening groups:** Create balance in a conversation or discussion.

- **Interest-based groups:** Take students preferences or selections into consideration to ensure the group can approach a task through a lens of interest.

¤ **Random groups:** Mix students up for tasks that may not benefit from a particular grouping strategy.

- Decide on a strategy for transitions. Find a cue (audio or visual) to signal the end of a rotation, then have a consistent method for transitioning students. For example, you can use a simple 1-2-3 strategy.

  1. **"Wrap up and clean up."** Give students a minute to get to a stopping spot and tidy up their stations.

  2. **"Stand behind your chair."** When students have their belongings packed up and are ready to rotate, they stand quietly behind their chairs, waiting to transition. This puts visual pressure on students who are moving more slowly.

  3. **"Transition."** Students should walk to the next station. Elementary students will benefit from practicing walking the path from one station to another to ensure they know where to go.

- Project a timer onto your board so students can keep track of the time as they work.

- Make sure every station displays clear directions. Using video directions may be more effective than lengthy typed instructions for online tasks or younger learners.

- Have a strategy ready for students who are having an off day or are distracting their peers. This can be as simple as positioning a couple of desks alongside a wall or near your teacher-led station where students can work in isolation if they are struggling to stay on task or disrupting other stations.

- Put a next steps or may-do protocol in place so students know what they should do when they are done. You can create a simple list on the board of items students can complete if they pace through the work more quickly than their peers.

- Give yourself permission *not* to grade everything students do in stations.

Table 3.2 (page 58) reviews differentiation and personalization, student agency, and student control over the time, place, pace, and path of learning in a station rotation lesson.

Table 3.2: Maximizing the Benefits of the Station Rotation Model

Key Benefits of Blended Learning	Ideas for Implementation
Differentiation and Personalization	• Strategic groupings allow for differentiated instruction. • Mixed skill-level groups require a variety of scaffolds and supports to be available for students to select from depending on their skills, abilities, needs, and preferences. • Online stations can be personalized using adaptive software and online programs. • Teachers can provide personalized feedback on work in progress at the teacher-led station.

Student Agency	• Teachers can build meaningful choices into a learning activity, allowing students to decide:
	   ¤ How to engage with information (for example, article, video, or podcast)
	   ¤ How they prefer to work (for example, alone, with a partner, or in a small group)
	   ¤ How they want to express their learning (for example, video recording, writing, or concept map)
	• Teachers can invite students to select a couple of stations to visit instead of requiring them to spend time at every station, or they can offer optional skill stations.

Student Control Over Time, Place, Pace, and Path	• Students can control the pace at which they process information or navigate tasks at stations that are not teacher led. • Students may also have some control over their learning paths if there are meaningful choices built into the learning experience that allow them to decide where to spend their time and energy. • Teachers can personalize individual students' learning paths with online resources or a digital curriculum as well as by allowing students the agency to make key decisions about their learning.

The station rotation model may be the most straightforward model for elementary teachers to begin with because they more frequently use learning centers or stations in their classrooms.

The Whole-Group Rotation Model

In the *whole-group rotation model*, the entire class rotates between online and offline learning activities. Traditional whole-group, teacher-led lessons require students to work on the same task simultaneously, and the teacher usually determines the pace of the lesson. By contrast, the goal of whole-group rotation, as with all blended learning models, is to give students agency, differentiate or personalize elements of the lesson, and provide students with control over the pace at which they consume new information or navigate tasks. Whole-group rotation also encourages you to pair each learning activity with the best learning landscape for that activity—online or offline—as well as to determine whether the task would benefit from being an individual or collaborative endeavor.

When Should You Use the Whole-Group Rotation Model?

You may want to consider a whole-group rotation if any of the following apply to you.

- **You teach in a 1:1 classroom:** Whole-group rotation works when there are enough devices for all students to work online simultaneously.

- **You are used to traditional instruction:** If you are comfortable with a whole-group, teacher-led lesson design but want to transition to blended learning models, whole-group rotation is a good place to start.

- **You want to engage the entire class:** Whole-group rotation is useful for whole-group offline activities that may generate noise and would not work in a small-group dynamic (such as a review game). Another example would be a lesson in which you want to present the same instruction or model for all students in the form of a minilesson.

- **You want to spend time with individual students:** Whole-group rotation creates time during the online learning activity to pull individual students for personalized instruction, reteaching, coaching, support, or conferencing.

- **Your class is small:** Whole-group rotation works well for classes that are too small to create stations (such as a special education class).

It's important to note that this model requires that all students have access to their own device for the online learning portions of the lesson, which may present a barrier if you do not teach in a school where every student has a device.

What Does the Whole-Group Rotation Model Look Like in Action?

Let's walk through an example of whole-group rotation to explore what is possible with this model. We'll use the whole-group rotation template pictured in figure 3.5 (page 60) to guide this example. However, it is important to note that there are myriad ways to combine online and offline learning in a whole-group rotation.

In this lesson, students enter the room and are presented with a hook activity to pique their interest in the topic that they'll be learning about in the lesson. For example, you can strategically pair or group students and present them with a mathematics puzzle to solve. Alternatively, you might pull all the students together and read a story or show part of a TED Talk to grab their interest.

Target standard or standards:			
Learning objectives or goals:			
	Time (minutes)	Activity description	Teacher focus
Offline learning activity: • Hook activity • Small-group discussion • Anticipatory set			
Online learning activity: • Listen to a story or podcast • Watch a video • Practice with an online program or adaptive software			
Teacher-led offline learning activity: • Direct instruction • I do, we do, groups do, you do • Facilitate a discussion			
"Would you rather?": Online or offline, individual or collaborative: • Practice and review • Problem solving • Apply and extend			
Exit activity: • Exit ticket • 3-2-1 • Reflection			

FIGURE 3.5: Whole-group rotation template.

Visit **go.SolutionTree.com/technology** *for a free reproducible version of this figure.*

Then the class transitions online to learn more about the lesson's topic. You may allow students the opportunity to decide whether they'd like to read an article, listen to a student-friendly podcast, or watch a video to learn about a topic. Allowing learners agency when it comes to how they engage with new information online can help eliminate barriers that make it hard for them to consume and process new information. There may also be students in the classroom who would benefit from working directly with you during this time instead of self-pacing through information online.

Once students have had time to explore an online resource, you can pull them back together for a debrief or discussion about what they discovered or learned. You may also want to use this time to complement the online information with additional direct instruction or a modeling session to introduce a new skill or strategy. During this teacher-led time, you can work with the class as a unit, but it is vital to keep these moments from consuming too much time in the lesson.

Again, the class can transition to the next activity to take what students learned from their work online and the teacher-led instruction or modeling session and attempt to do something with that new information, strategy, or skill. This is another opportunity for meaningful choice. Perhaps students can decide if they prefer to practice offline with pencil and paper or online with a review program. Maybe they have the chance to work alone, with a partner, or as part of a small group to apply what they learned. These choices built into the parts of a whole-group rotation allow students to select options that will enable them to navigate the task successfully.

Finally, you can end the lesson with an exit ticket to collect information about what students now know or encourage a short reflective practice. This provides useful formative assessment data you can use to see how successful the lesson was at meeting the intended learning objectives.

Let's explore an example (figure 3.6, page 62). This is what the lesson I have described in this section might look like in practice.

How Can You Ensure a Whole-Group Rotation Lesson Runs Smoothly?

The following pointers will help you keep the right things in mind as you implement the whole-group rotation model.

- Balance the online tasks with the offline tasks and the individual tasks with the collaborative tasks in the design of your whole-group rotation.

- Use the online learning activities to allow for personalization through the software you use to engage students online or by pulling individual learners for personalized coaching and support during the online learning activities.

- Embrace a "Would you rather?" mentality in your design work and see if you can give students at least one meaningful choice during your whole-group rotation.

Whole-Group Rotation: Mathematics Lesson	Time (Minutes)	Activity Description	Teacher Focus
Offline learning activity	Ten	Present an unfamiliar mathematics problem, pair or group students strategically, and allow time for them to think critically, engage in conversation, and work collaboratively to try to sove the problem.	Listen and observe to identify strong strategies that students use and misconceptions or areas of confusion to address.
Online learning activity	Fifteen	Provide a collection of resources for students to explore to understand how to solve this type of problem (for example, videos, text, and an interactive website) and capture their notes in a graphic organizer or guided note template.	Pull a group of students who would benefit from support in navigating online resources.
Teacher-led learning activity	Fifteen	Move students through an I do, we do, groups do, you do progression to help them solve this type of problem.	Begin by modeling and guiding the group through a we do segment. Then, during the groups do, observe to identify students who are not prepared for independent practice and need more time with the teacher (for example, additional instruction, modeling, or scaffolds) before transitioning to the you do.
"Would you rather?"... online or offline	Ten	Students can continue practicing online with a program like Khan Academy (www.khanacademy.org), IXL (www.ixl.com), or Desmos, or offline with pencil and paper. They can choose to work on their own or with a partner.	Lend additional support to students who are struggling or have questions.
Exit activity	Five	Students complete an online or offline exit ticket designed to check for understanding, reflect on the lesson, or both.	Analyze the data to understand how effective the lesson was at meeting stated learning objectives.

FIGURE 3.6: Whole-group rotation example.

- Be strategic about what you are asking students to do online versus what they are doing offline. Are you choosing the best learning environment for the activity?

Table 3.3 reviews differentiation and personalization, student agency, and student control over the time, place, pace, and path of learning in a whole-group rotation lesson.

Table 3.3: Maximizing the Benefits of the Whole-Group Rotation Model

Key Benefits of Blended Learning	Ideas for Implementation
Differentiation and Personalization	• Strategic pairing and groupings during online and offline tasks allow for peer support. • Online learning activities can be personalized using adaptive software and online programs. • The teacher can provide differentiated or personalized instruction and support by pulling small groups or individual students during online learning sections of the lesson.

Student Agency	• Teachers can build "Would you rather?" choices into the offline and online learning activities to allow students to make decisions about their learning. For example, Would you rather:
	  ¤ Work alone, with a partner, or as part of a small group?
	  ¤ Participate in a live small-group discussion or share your thoughts in an online asynchronous discussion?
	  ¤ Make connections in writing or fill in a concept map?

Student Control Over Time, Place, Pace, and Path	• Teachers can personalize individual students' learning paths with online resources or a digital curriculum as well as by allowing students the agency to make key decisions about their learning.

The whole-group rotation model may be the most manageable blended learning model for secondary teachers to experiment with first because it is the closest to the whole-group, teacher-led lesson.

The Flipped Classroom Model

The *flipped classroom model* inverts the traditional approach to instruction and application. Instead of spending large chunks of class time providing whole-group instruction, you record videos capturing your minilessons, short lectures, modeling sessions, and demonstrations. That way, students can self-pace through the recordings, pausing, rewinding, and rewatching as needed.

You can assign the video content for homework, use it to create an online station, or weave it into a whole-group rotation or the playlist model. Leveraging video frees you from the front of the room, allowing you to spend your precious class time facilitating learning and working directly with students to support practice and application.

When Should You Use the Flipped Classroom Model?

You may want to consider using the flipped classroom model if any of the following apply to you.

- **You want to focus on supporting individual students:** The flipped classroom model lends itself to less time at the front of the room transferring information and more time working directly with individual students or small groups.

- **You plan to provide the same instruction, explanation, model, or demonstration for the entire class:** With the flipped classroom model, you can use the same content, which is useful for times when you don't need to differentiate the instructional experience or when you find you're repeating the same instructional pieces.

- **You want to increase accessibility for students:** The flipped classroom model is ideal for students who struggle to stay attentive or take notes during live instruction. Allowing them to manipulate the speed of the video or adding closed captioning improves accessibility. Students working asynchronously from home on a hybrid schedule also benefit from this model.

What Does the Flipped Classroom Model Look Like in Action?

Video is most effective when it is woven into a complete blended learning experience. You can follow a three-step process.

1. Pre-video activity
2. Video lesson
3. Post-video activity

Table 3.4 offers more details, and the following sections explain each in turn.

STEP 1: PRE-VIDEO ACTIVITY

The pre-video activity can be an individual or a collaborative task depending on the objectives. For example, suppose the goal is to get your students to access and share their prior knowledge. For example, a history teacher who plans to introduce the concept of democracy may begin by asking students what they think that word means and where that prior knowledge comes from. Whereas a physical education teacher introducing students to a style of dance might want to preteach key vocabulary relating to specific movements common to that style of dance. This can help remove barriers in the lesson to ensure students understand the content presented in the video. In that case, an individual reflection or a small-group discussion (online or offline) are effective strategies. However, you may want to begin the lesson with a collaborative task since the experience of watching the actual video will be an individual endeavor.

Table 3.4: Designing a Three-Part Flipped Lesson

Pre-Video Activity	<ul><li>Pique student interest.</li><ul><li>Use a story, video clip, puzzle, student-friendly podcast, political cartoon, or game to pique student interest.</li></ul><li>Assess prior knowledge.</li><ul><li>Engage students in a discussion or use a writing prompt to get them accessing and sharing their prior knowledge.</li><ul><li>What do students know about this topic?</li><li>Where did they learn it?</li></ul></ul><li>Drive inquiry or surface wonderings.</li><ul><li>Engage students in a brainstorming activity, or use a thinking routine like "See/Think/Wonder" (Project Zero, 2019c; see chapter 7, page 152).</li></ul><li>Present students with an unfamiliar problem, task, or challenge to engage them in a collaborative problem-solving activity.</li></ul>
Video Lesson	<ul><li>Build an interactive lesson around the video content using a tool like Edpuzzle (https://edpuzzle.com), Playposit (https://go.playposit.com), or Screencastify (www.screencastify.com).</li><ul><li>What questions can you drop into the video lesson to check for understanding or drive higher-order thinking?</li></ul><li>Provide students with a concept map or guided note template to fill in as they watch the video.</li><ul><li>How can you help students to identify the critical information in the video and capture their thinking?</li></ul><li>Pair the video with a set of questions or an online discussion prompt in your learning management system.</li><ul><li>What can you ask to encourage students to think more deeply about the video content?</li></ul></ul>
Post-Video Activity	<ul><li>Draw a sketchnote (visual note taking), mind map, or flowchart surfacing the big concepts presented in the video and showing their connections or relationships to one another.</li><ul><li>Can you give students the agency to decide how they want to surface their learning visually?</li></ul><li>Provide practice problems.</li><li>Review with online software.</li><li>Work with manipulatives.</li><li>Provide a writing prompt or task.</li><li>Implement a collaborative group challenge.</li><ul><li>How can you engage groups of students to work collaboratively to transfer their learning to a novel situation?</li></ul></ul>

STEP 2: VIDEO LESSON

During the second part of the three-part flipped lesson, students watch *and* engage with the video. The students' engagement with the video is critical to ensure that they do not slip into a passive, consumptive role while viewing the video. The goal of this engagement activity is two-fold. First, it encourages students to think critically about the information presented in the video. This will aid their comprehension and retention. Second, the engagement task provides evidence of completion. You may be hesitant to use video because you are worried about accountability. How will you know if students watched the video? If you ask students to complete a task paired with the video, that task becomes evidence of completion. The history teacher doing the lesson on democracy might use a Crash Course (https://bit.ly/3Bw8er9) video on democracy and pair it with a concept map or use a program like Edpuzzle to drop questions in to the video to check for understanding. By contrast, the physical education teacher might record a video to demonstrate specific dances and model the correct movements. As students watch, they can take guided notes or draw sketch-notes (see page 181) of specific dance moves.

If they watch the video in class as part of a whole-group rotation instead of at home as part of an online assignment, you will need to build a buffer of time around the video. When you use video instruction in the classroom, students no longer control the elements of time and place; however, they should still have some control over the pace at which they consume and process the new information. They must have enough time to pause and rewind the video to ensure they understand the content. A good rule of thumb is to double the time of the video and give students that length of time to complete the video lesson. If the video is six minutes, you will want to give students a minimum of twelve minutes. However, if you ask students to answer multiple questions as they watch the video, you'll want to extend the time for the video portion of the lesson, so students are not rushed.

STEP 3: POST-VIDEO ACTIVITY

The post-video activity should challenge students to take what they learned in the video and do something with it. You can follow the video with practice to review key concepts, challenge students to surface their learning visually or artistically, or engage the group in a discussion or collaborative challenge to learn with and from each other.

This final step in the lesson presents another opportunity to incorporate student agency by presenting students with a choice of follow-up activities. For example, you can let students decide which strategy they want to use to surface their learning visually: mind map, sketchnote, or flowchart. You can let them decide whether or not they want to review vocabulary, concepts, or problems offline with a handout or online with adaptive software. You can give them the choice of whether they work alone, with a partner, or in a group. Giving students an option at this moment in the lesson can increase the likelihood that they will stay engaged in the task (Schneider, Nebel, Beege, & Rey, 2018). For example, the history teacher could follow the video with small-group discussions or a collaborative research assignment into democratic governments around the world to deepen their understanding of this concept. The physical education teacher might have pairs or groups of students practice specific dance moves, then record short videos showing specific movements using FlipGrid, where they can receive both teacher and peer feedback.

As students practice and apply, your focus should be on listening, observing, and collecting formative assessment data. Which students might need additional support or scaffolds to be successful? Are there students who would benefit from working directly with you so that you can guide their practice? This is an opportunity for you to read the room and figure out who successfully navigates the task and who might need additional instruction. Then you can spend your valuable class time supporting individuals or small groups of learners.

Use the template pictured in figure 3.7 to design a dynamic learning experience around video content.

Step 1: Pre-Video Activity	Step 2: Video Lesson	Step 3: Post-Video Activity
Drive Inquiry, Pique Interest, Access Prior Knowledge, or Preteach Vocabulary How can you create some context for the video students will watch?	Transfer Information and Engage How will you drive engagement and higher-order thinking around the video content?	Extend and Apply How will you ask students to apply what they learned?
Activity description:	Activity description:	Activity description:
What materials or technology tools do you need for this step?	What materials or technology tools do you need for this step?	What materials or technology tools do you need for this step?
To do:	To do:	To do:

FIGURE 3.7: Three-part flipped lesson template.

*Visit **go.SolutionTree.com/technology** for a free reproducible version of this figure.*

How Can You Ensure a Flipped Classroom Lesson Runs Smoothly?

The following pointers will help you keep the right things in mind as you implement the flipped classroom model.

- Keep your videos short (a helpful rule is one minute per grade level in school; see page 83) to maintain student engagement with the video content.

- When making your videos, include relevant visuals (such as images, charts, or maps) to help students understand the content.

- Always ask students to do something as they watch the video (such as answer questions or complete a guided note template or concept map).

- Build a complete learning experience around the video content (that is, pre- and post-video activities) to maximize the effectiveness of videos.

- If students watch a video in class, build a buffer of time around the video lesson to ensure students have time to pause, rewind, and rewatch sections.

- Add closed captioning, if possible, to make your video more accessible.

- Use a formative assessment strategy to assess the video's effectiveness in helping students understand key concepts or apply specific skills. These data will help you identify students who need additional instruction and support.

Table 3.5 reviews differentiation and personalization, student agency, and student control over the time, place, pace, and path of learning in a flipped classroom lesson.

The Playlist (or Individual Rotation) Model

The *playlist model* is a sequence of learning activities designed to move students toward a clear objective or desired outcome. Teachers can use a playlist to teach a concept, strategy, skill, process, or walk students through the parts of a multistep performance task or project. You can create a playlist inside of your LMS or in a digital document using a template like the one pictured in figure 3.8 (page 70).

The playlist model shifts control over the pace of learning to the students, so they work well for learning that benefits from student control over the pace of learning and variable time on task. While your students self-pace through the parts of a playlist, you can focus on supporting individual or small groups of learners in the form of teacher check-ins or conferencing sessions. This structure also creates time for you to assess students one by one with them sitting next to you (side-by-side assessments) as the final check-in.

Table 3.5: Maximizing the Benefits of the Flipped Classroom Model

Key Benefits of Blended Learning	Ideas for Implementation

Differentiation and Personalization	• The teacher can differentiate the pre- and post-video learning activities for students at different levels of readiness.
	   ¤ Pre-video activity
	   ¤ Engagement with the video
	   ¤ Post-video activity
	• The teacher can pull individual students to provide personalized support as they attempt to apply what they learned in part 3.

Student Agency	• Students may have the opportunity to decide how they want to apply what they learned in the post-video activity.
Student Control Over Time, Place, Pace, and Path	• If the teacher sends the video content home with students in the form of homework, then students control the time, place, and pace of their experience. • If the video content is part of the in-class lesson, students have control over the pace of their learning.

When Should You Use the Playlist Model?

You may want to consider the playlist model if any of the following apply to you.

- **The lesson you are teaching would benefit from variable time on task and personalization:** When students are completing, for example, a multistep task, project, or formal writing assignment, the playlist model gives them control over the pace at which they progress through the various steps in the process and access to teacher support as they work.

- **You want to focus your time and energy on supporting individual learners:** The playlist model frees you from the front of the room because the playlist supplies everything students need, such as directions, models, links to resources, activities, and so on. You can provide additional instruction and support via the teacher check-ins built into the playlist. These informal conferences make it possible to modify or adjust students' playlists as they work to personalize their experience and ensure they continue making progress.

What Does the Playlist Model Look Like in Action?

Teachers typically build the actual playlist using features in an LMS, a digital document, or a slide deck. The playlist presents a sequential order of learning activities that students self-pace to complete. When students are working on a playlist in the

Playlist: _____

This playlist is designed to _____.
Follow the directions for each activity and complete the items in order.

Activity	Directions	Notes	Date Completed
1. *Example:* View requirements of this playlist.	*Example:* Watch this **screencast** that reviews the requirements of this playlist. Post your questions in the Notes column.		
2.			
3.			
4.			
Teacher check-in 1: Provide support and personalize instruction			
5.			
6.			
7.			
8.			
Teacher check-in 2: Discuss progress and provide feedback			
9.			
10.			
11.			
12.			
Final teacher check-in: Conduct side-by-side assessments			

FIGURE 3.8: Playlist model template.

*Visit **go.SolutionTree.com/technology** for a free reproducible version of this figure.*

classroom, teachers may position them at individual desks, arrange them in pairs, or seat them in small groups. Although progress through a playlist is individual, pairing or grouping students for peer support can be a helpful strategy to ensure students have a network of classmates they can lean on if they hit a bump while the teacher is occupied with another student. As students work on their playlists, the teacher is positioned at a desk in the classroom to facilitate check-ins.

Let's explore an example. An English teacher might create a novel study playlist. Given the diversity of reading levels in the classroom, the novel study playlist may include the same standards-aligned tasks, but students at different reading levels may read texts that are accessible to them or in a genre of interest. Despite reading different novels, students will all complete the same standards-aligned tasks associated with their specific text. For example, they may have to identify a central theme, create detailed character profiles, use context clues to define unfamiliar words, and analyze the text for explicit and implicit information. In a traditional class, all students would read the same book on the same time line and complete the same tasks. A novel study playlist would allow students to read a book appropriate to their reading level, and enjoy more control over the pace at which they read their book and complete the various standard-aligned learning activities. Students read their texts and work through their individual playlists at a pace that works for them. Then, when they hit teacher check-ins at strategic moments in their playlist, they join a queue to conference with the teacher about their progress. A novel study playlist would also allow teachers to meet with individual or small groups of learners to review their work, identify gaps or misconceptions, and provide additional reteaching, feedback, and support. During the teacher check-ins, you have the opportunity to make adjustments or additions to each student's playlist to personalize their paths based on formative assessment data and the conversations with the student.

How Can You Ensure a Playlist Lesson Runs Smoothly?

The following pointers will help you keep the right things in mind as you implement the playlist model.

- Mix media and learning modalities (such as visual, auditory, and tactile) to keep students engaged and interested.

- Blend online and offline learning activities so students get a break from the screen and have opportunities to engage in tactile, experiential, and social learning.

- Include scaffolds and supports in the playlist to ensure students have what they need to be successful (for example, graphic organizers, links to vocabulary videos, sentence frames, or deconstructed models).

- Establish clear expectations about how students signal they are ready for their teacher check-in (for example, send a message via LMS, submit a request via a digital form, or place a sticky note on the board) and what they should do if they are ready to meet but you are occupied with another student (such as working on a may-do activity).

- Build mechanisms into the playlist to collect formative assessment data. This will be helpful during teacher check-ins to assess student progress and make the necessary adjustments to the playlist.

- Be strategic about when and where you place your teacher check-ins. Ideally, these are moments when students would benefit from personalized instruction, support, or feedback. Too many check-ins will create a backlog of students waiting to conference, while too few check-ins will leave students feeling unsure of their progress.

- Arrange students in pairs or groups to provide peer support as they progress through the playlist. Their partner or group should be their first point of contact if they have a question or hit a bump.

Table 3.6 reviews differentiation and personalization, student agency, and student control over the time, place, pace, and path of learning while working through a playlist.

Table 3.6: Maximizing the Benefits of the Playlist Model

Key Benefits of Blended Learning	Ideas for Implementation
Differentiation and Personalization	· When designing a playlist, teachers can differentiate by making a few versions of the playlist. 　¤ Middle-of-the-road playlist 　¤ Advanced version with more academically rigorous practice and fewer teacher check-ins 　¤ Scaffolded version with more video instruction, embedded supports, and teacher check-ins · Teachers can personalize individual playlists during the teacher check-ins when they review the formative assessment data, discuss the student's progress, and customize the path to ensure each student continues making progress.
Student Agency	· The playlist should include meaningful choices. Teachers can include "Would you rather?" options in a playlist to allow students to decide how they want to engage with information, process or practice what they are learning, and demonstrate their learning.
Student Control Over Time, Place, Pace, and Path	· Students have control over the pace at which they complete learning activities. · Students may also have some control over their learning paths if there are substantive choices woven into the design of the playlist.

The playlist should be a one-stop shop with everything students need to work independently (such as directions, instruction, and resources). This requires significant planning time, since you are putting all the pieces in place in advance. However, the time investment on the front end pays dividends during class time because you can monitor progress, provide feedback, and assess student work during your teacher check-ins instead of taking that work home to do in your evenings and on weekends.

Other Models

The taxonomy of blended learning models moves from one end of a spectrum—where the teacher is the driver, playing a critical role in designing, instructing, and facilitating learning—to the opposite end of the spectrum, where the models rely more heavily on online learning as the driver. That means the students are working through a robust online curriculum, so teachers are not designing or instructing. Instead, they focus more on facilitating learning and monitoring student progress. The flex, a la carte, and enriched virtual models demand significant financial investment in an online curriculum, which individual teachers do not have control over. An investment like that happens at a district level. These models are often used to offer an alternative to traditional courses for students who are not thriving in a traditional school setting.

Flex Model

The flex model is similar to the rotation models in that learning takes place in a traditional school environment. However, unlike the rotation models, the flex model relies more heavily on technology-rich instruction, which requires that schools invest in an online learning provider or a robust and comprehensive online curriculum.

The goal of the flex model is to provide learners with a personalized learning path that they can self-pace through with the support of an onsite teacher. The flex model positions teachers to spend their time providing individuals and small groups of learners with additional instruction, supports and scaffolds, and feedback on work in progress (Staker & Horn, 2012; Yang, Zhu, & MacLeod, 2016).

A la Carte Model

The a la cart model is an entirely online course that complements, supplements, or runs parrallel to the student's traditional face-to-face classes. For example, students might take a course for credit recovery because they failed the course the first time they took it and need the credit to graduate. Alternatively, some students may take an online course because the class they want is not offered on campus. For example, a student who wants to take an advanced math course, which is not available face-to-face, may enroll in that class online. Students may work on these courses entirely asynchronously from home or work at a computer lab on campus during their school day. If students need help or support, they access the teacher of record online (Staker & Horn, 2012; Yang et al., 2016).

Enriched Virtual Model

The enriched virtual model is a departure from the normal school schedule because students learn primarily online as they self-pace through an education program. They meet periodically with the teacher of record to conference, or come to school to participate in hands-on learning experiences like labs and experiments. This model relies heavily on the online delivery of instruction and content, allowing for a high degree of autonomy (Staker & Horn, 2012; Yang et al., 2016).

Wrap-Up and Next Steps

The diversity of learners in a classroom and the range of standards educators are responsible for teaching demand a flexible approach to design. Just as a single tool cannot solve every problem, the same instructional model will not work for all students or every learning objective. Teachers need a collection of models to choose from when designing learning experiences that position the students as active agents in the learning process.

Think big, but start small. Select a single model to experiment with, and know that you're going to make mistakes. That's OK. Mistakes are part of the learning process. Over time, you'll develop confidence in your understanding of each model's benefits, what they look like in action, what your role is in that model, and how to maximize the effectiveness of the model by prioritizing student agency, differentiation and personalization, and student control over the pace of learning. As you develop higher levels of self-efficacy with one model, you can begin to experiment with another. The goal is to build on a series of small successes over time.

A transition away from reliance on the whole-group, teacher-led model to blended learning is a journey. It takes time, experimentation, practice, failure, and refinement.

If you see yourself as the lead learner in the classroom, you know learning has no end point. This mentality can, in turn, inspire students in their learning journeys. Instead, you can enjoy the process of expanding your skill set over time and eventually get to a point where you can be nimble in your work as a designer, or architect, of learning experiences.

Consider taking the following next steps as a way to further what you've learned. See also the reflection questions on page 76.

- Select one of the blended learning models I describe in this chapter, and design a lesson for your students. Think about the objectives of the lesson. What do you want students to know, understand, or be able to do at the end of this lesson? How much support are they going to need to make progress toward this objective? Are they more likely to successfully meet this objective if they work alone, with a partner, in small groups, or in a dynamic of their choice? Once you have spent time considering the answers to these questions, make sure the model you have selected is a good match for the objectives you've identified.

- Use the template provided for the blended learning model you selected to design a learning experience that includes at least one of the following: student agency, differentiation, and some control over the pace of learning.

- Review the tips for making this particular model run smoothly. Consider which you need to spend time thinking about in advance of facilitating this lesson with your students. Are there protocols, procedures, workflow considerations, grouping strategies, and so on that you need to have to ensure that your students will be successful?

- Share your lesson plan with a colleague for feedback and make any necessary adjustments to your lesson.

Chapter 3: Teachers as Designers of Learning Experiences—Reflect and Discuss

I encourage you to pause here to reflect on or discuss the following questions. If you are reading this book on your own, you can reflect on these questions in a blog post, publish your thoughts on your favorite social media platform, or capture your thoughts in a journal or notebook. If you are reading this book as part of a book club or book study, use the following questions to facilitate vibrant in-person or online discussions.

1. Which instructional models are you currently using? What are the benefits and limitations of these models? How much control do your students currently have over the time, place, path, and pace of their learning?

2. Of the four blended learning rotation models I describe in this chapter, which are you most drawn to as a place to start? Why is this model appealing? What would this model allow you to spend your time doing in the lesson? What concerns do you have about using this model? Which of the tips about making this model run smoothly resonated with you?

3. Review table 3.1 (page 54; Ideas for Designing Stations in a Station Rotation Lesson). Given your grade level, content area, and population of students, what specific strategies could you use to engage your students at these three stations? What might the station activities described (for example, building background, practice and review, or collaborative problem solving) look like in your classroom?

The Complete Guide to Blended Learning © 2022 Solution Tree Press • SolutionTree.com
Visit **go.SolutionTree.com/technology** to download this free reproducible.

4. How do you currently provide students with agency or the opportunity to make key decisions about their learning? What does this look like in your classroom? How might using these various blended learning models help you prioritize student agency? What are your thoughts on starting simple with a "Would you rather?" approach to agency, building at least one meaningful choice into each lesson? Brainstorm a list of "Would you rather?" options that you could apply to a variety of lessons. For example, Would you rather work alone or with a partner? Would you rather participate in a live discussion or post your thoughts to an asynchronous online discussion?

5. What do you spend the most time repeating, re-explaining, or reteaching each year? Which concepts, explanations, instruction, and models do students typically need repeated exposure to? What are your thoughts on building a three-part flipped lesson to design a complete learning experience around video content and ensure students stay actively engaged when watching video content? How can you use the pre- and post-video activities to prioritize offline learning and foster collaboration?

6. Since the playlist model shifts control over the pace of learning to the students, think about concepts, skills, processes, or projects that might work well in this format. How might you structure a playlist to ensure students can successfully navigate the learning activities? Would you pair or group students strategically for peer support? How might you use your teacher check-ins to support your students as they work? What norms or expectations would you establish to ensure students transition to and from the teacher check-ins smoothly?

CHAPTER 4

TEACHERS AS INSTRUCTORS AND CONNECTORS

When I stepped into my first classroom in 2001, I believed I had to be the expert on everything. The prospect of not knowing the answer to a question was terrifying. I thought that my content-area expertise was the value I brought into the classroom. I was supposed to be a fountain of knowledge that students could count on to have all the answers, yet I was keenly aware that I did not know everything. I was learning one step ahead of my students in those early years.

As I reflect on my experience, I realize that this misconception that teachers' value lies in their content-area expertise likely stems from the reality that before technology permeated classrooms, the teacher and the textbook were the sole sources of information. If teachers couldn't answer a question, they couldn't pull out a phone or open a laptop to do a quick online search. It makes sense that teachers preparing to enter classrooms before the digital revolution felt like their role as the instructor was paramount.

Luckily for new teachers today, technology has changed all of that. There's much less pressure to know it all. There isn't any shame in saying, "I don't know. Let's figure it out." In my experience as a teacher and coach, that honest response can actually help students feel more empowered to admit when they are not sure about something and encourages them to be curious problem solvers.

Unfortunately, there are still many teachers who feel that their value lies in their expertise. That belief manifests as a lot of teacher-talk and whole-group, teacher-led lessons. It is often those same teachers who feel threatened by technology and blended learning. If we as teachers believe our value is a product of our expertise, then technology is scary. Google will *always* know more than us on just about every searchable topic. So, our value can no longer be tied to our expertise. Instead, we have to appreciate that our actual value lies in our ability to connect with learners. It is the human side of teaching that technology can never replace.

The more time teachers spend talking, the less time students have to engage with the content and with each other. Traditional modes of instruction place the focus on the teacher. By contrast, blended learning aims to shift the focus to the students and give them control over their learning experience, as shown in figure 4.1.

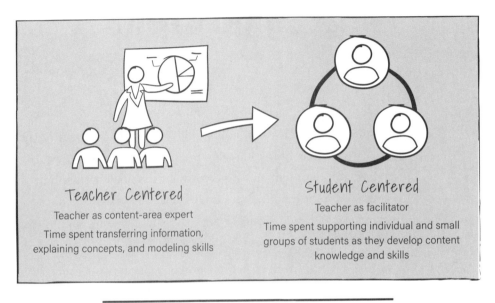

Teacher Centered

Teacher as content-area expert

Time spent transferring information, explaining concepts, and modeling skills

Student Centered

Teacher as facilitator

Time spent supporting individual and small groups of students as they develop content knowledge and skills

FIGURE 4.1: From expert to connector.

My goal when working with educators is to encourage them to think critically about how to use their time with students and what mode of instruction will yield the best learning outcomes. How can we use instruction to shift the focus from the teacher to the learner? How can we make time to shift from talking at students and telling them what we know about a topic to connecting with them and supporting them as they develop content knowledge and hone skills?

> We have to appreciate that our actual value lies in our ability to connect with learners. It is the human side of teaching that technology can never replace.

In this chapter, I'll focus on some ways to accomplish this. First, I'll discuss the differences between asynchronous and synchronous instruction, then explain how to leverage asynchronous video instruction for student success, and finally provide strategies for structuring synchronous instruction for small groups.

The Difference Between Asynchronous and Synchronous Instruction

There are two modes of instruction in a blended learning or online learning environment: (1) asynchronous and (2) synchronous. With *asynchronous instruction*, learning takes place at different times, and the learner may control the time, place, and pace of the experience. Teachers generally engage in asynchronous instruction using video, which students can pause, rewind, or rewatch as needed.

By contrast, *synchronous instruction* happens in a specific time and place, often with limited opportunities for students to control the pace of that experience. However, teachers are present to support the process when instruction is live. They can differentiate that experience by providing support and scaffolds and strategically pairing or grouping students to encourage peer support as students process, practice, and apply the learning.

Synchronous instruction can take place with the entire class as part of a whole-group rotation or in the form of small-group differentiated instruction as part of a station rotation lesson. By contrast, asynchronous instruction is the cornerstone of the flipped classroom model and plays a critical role in the playlist or individual rotation model, providing on-demand teaching and modeling. Table 4.1 (page 82) lists the benefits of each type of instruction.

The question most teachers ask is, "When should I make a video, and when should I pull the instruction into our live sessions?" The answer is that if they are planning to say the same thing in the same way to all students, then I would recommend making a video. Video is perfect for those foundational explanations or models that *all* students need to hear and see. Students often need to hear foundational explanations about key concepts, strategies, and skills repeatedly. Even though it takes time to create a video, those videos pay dividends, saving teachers precious instructional time throughout a unit, learning cycle, trimester, or semester. They are also resources teachers can use from year to year. Additionally, if teachers spend less time on these basic explanations, they can spend more time supporting learners in teacher-led, small-group sessions.

Table 4.1: Benefits of Asynchronous and Synchronous Instruction

Asynchronous	Synchronous
• Students control the pace at which they consume and process information. • Video instruction can support learners and their families when students are learning remotely. • As teachers create video content, they build a repository of on-demand resources that students can refer to repeatedly throughout the school year. • Students who transfer into a class midyear or miss class due to an extended absence can access the instruction they missed. • Using video can free the teacher from feeling trapped at the front of the room and create more time for connection in a classroom.	• Teachers can differentiate the experience by adjusting examples and models for students at different levels and providing additional supports and scaffolds (such as sentence frames, guided note templates, concept maps, other examples, or access to visuals) to meet individual learners where they are. • Teachers can facilitate the experience to drive more in-depth thinking and support student progress. • Teachers can engage students directly in thinking about and discussing key concepts to ensure they understand the new information. • Teachers can structure their live sessions to engage learners in conversation and practice, making it possible to collect formative assessment data about the progress of each student.

Effective Asynchronous Video Instruction

Video is versatile and can be used for a range of different purposes, including the following.

- Transferring information (for example, minilessons, short lectures, and brief explanations)
- Modeling (for example, demonstrating a process, conducting a think-aloud, and onboarding students to a new routine or technology tool)
- Providing directions or how-to tutorials (for example, step-by-step instructions about how to complete an assignment or task)
- Providing remediation or reteaching teachers who have never created video content before may feel daunted by the process and unsure of where to start.

There are several questions, which I address in the following sections, that you should consider as you begin makeing video content.

- How long should my videos be?
- How can I create effective video content?
- What process should I use to make my first instructional video?

How Long Should My Videos Be?

Researchers Philip J. Guo, Juho Kim, and Rob Rubin (2014) conducted an empirical study on video engagement that identifies video length as the most significant factor impacting student engagement with videos. The study concludes that shorter videos are more engaging, which is worth keeping in mind as you create your video content. A helpful guideline I use when coaching teachers is to limit video length to one minute of video content per year in school. For example, videos for third-grade students should be between three and four minutes in length. Videos for ninth-grade students should be nine to ten minutes. I have found this rule works well across grade levels.

> A helpful guideline to follow is one minute of video content per year in school.

How Can I Create Effective Video Content?

In her article on effective educational videos, science educator Cynthia Brame (2015) describes specific things that educators can do to improve the quality and effectiveness of their videos by minimizing students' cognitive loads. Brame (2015) recommends that educators consider the four practices shown in table 4.2 (page 84), which can increase the effectiveness of video content: (1) segmenting, (2) signaling, (3) weeding, and (4) matching modality.

What Process Should I Use to Make an Instructional Video?

Table 4.3 (page 85) describes a three-part process you can use to create video content. It is by no means the only strategy, but it does encourage a high level of intentionality around the design of the video content and gives teachers new to the process a place to start. This process also prioritizes the four considerations described in table 4.2 (page 84) for creating effective video content.

Table 4.2: Four Considerations for Teachers Creating Educational Videos

Four Considerations for Teachers Creating Educational Videos	
Segmenting	Chunk the presentation of new information into bite-sized pieces. It is always better to make a few shorter videos than one long video. • What specific idea, concept, skill, strategy, or process are you planning to focus on in your video?
Signaling and Cueing	Draw the student's eye to specific information in the video by underlining or highlighting keywords, phrases, or vocabulary and inserting an arrow or symbol to point to particular elements in your examples and media. • Can you use the animation feature of your presentation software or use specific colors on a recordable whiteboard? • Can you animate a bulleted list of information so that each bullet appears when you are ready to talk about it or show one problem at a time on a recordable whiteboard?
Weeding	Eliminate anything unnecessary, including busy backgrounds, themes, unrelated images, and unnecessary music or sounds. • Are your slides clear and straightforward? • If you plan to use a recordable whiteboard, can you storyboard in advance to ensure the visual side of your presentation is clear and organized?
Matching Modality	Think about aligning your visuals with your audio track. It helps students to see visual representations of what they are hearing. • What visuals can you incorporate into your video (for example, photographs, graphics, charts, and maps) to help students see what you are explaining?

Source: Adapted from Brame, 2015.

This approach to creating video content can help teachers who are new to the process of making instructional videos feel more confident as they work through a clear progression of steps to produce strong video content. However, this approach may not work for all content areas. For example, if you are a mathematics teacher, you may want to explore a recordable whiteboard, like Whiteboard (www.whiteboard .chat) or Educreations (www.educreations.com), as a strategy to make your videos. These are among the several online platforms that turn your tablet or devices into a *recordable whiteboard*, which allows teachers to draw images, diagrams, or mathematics problems, and record those drawings with a verbal explanation to make the video instruction easier to create for subjects that demand visual models and demonstrations. To prepare for a video using a recordable whiteboard, it's best to storyboard your content in advance to maximize the effectiveness and clarity of the presentation.

It is critical that you put aside any expectation that your videos will be perfect. Striving for perfection with a video is an exercise in frustration. The reality is that live

Table 4.3: Three-Step Process for Creating Video Content

Three-Step Process for Creating Video Content	
Step 1: Create Your Content in a Presentation	First, decide what the focus of your video will be. Since shorter videos are preferable, it's important to chunk the presentation of new information into bite-size pieces. Consider what concept, skill, strategy, process, or other content you will you focus on in this video.
	Next, create a presentation using Google Slides (www.google.com/slides), PowerPoint (https://bit.ly/3Fz9OZP), Keynote (www.apple.com/keynote), or other presentation software. Formatting your content in a presentation ahead of time helps you be more intentional in presenting the information. Consider the following.
	• What keywords or phrases will you need to include on your slides? Avoid adding too much verbiage, since you can expand on these keywords with your verbal explanation.
	• What media will help students see (understand) what you are explaining?
Step 2: Add Animation	Once your content is in place, use the animation feature of your presentation software to animate the following.
	• **The bulleted list:** That way, each bullet in the list appears separately, ensuring that students focus on the point you are making as you are explaining it.
	• **Arrows or visual markers:** These draw the students' eyes to specific aspects of the media you have included in your presentation.
Step 3: Record a Screencast	Finally, select a screencasting tool, like Screencastify (www.screencastify.com) or Loom (www.loom.com/screen-recorder), record your screen with the projected presentation, and capture the audio track of your explanation.
	If possible, add closed captioning to your videos to increase accessibility for students with hearing difficulties or who process text-based instruction more readily than verbal.

instruction isn't perfect. I am rarely as articulate as I would like to be when providing instruction, so I try not to put pressure on myself to make my videos perfect. If I stumble a little over my words or hit a minor technology hiccup, I try to keep going instead of stopping the video and starting over. It's vital that creating video content be a sustainable part of your practice. If we strive for perfection, we might find ourselves not using the strategy in the long term.

Strategies to Structure Synchronous Small-Group Instruction

As useful and versatile as video can be, it is not ideal for every situation. Small-group instruction is a critical part of any blended learning environment. If you shift the foundational explanations that you would typically present to the whole group online using video, you can reserve your precious small-group time for the following types of activities that maximize your time with students.

- Differentiated small-group instruction
- Interactive modeling sessions with problems or prompts at different levels of academic rigor
- Guided practice and application
- Real-time feedback on work in progress
- Small-group discussion of complex concepts, texts, issues, or video content

The station rotation model described in chapter 3 (page 47) provides a structure you can use to provide teacher-led, small-group learning experiences, as pictured in figure 4.2.

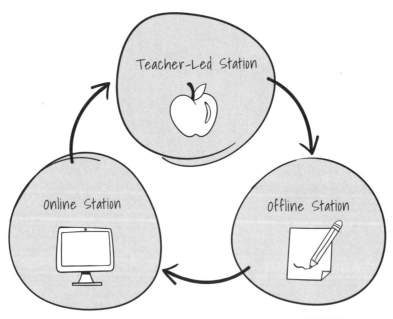

FIGURE 4.2: Teacher-led station for small-group instruction as part of a station rotation lesson.

The teacher-led station creates time in the lesson for you to work directly with small groups of learners to connect with them and better meet their needs. I encourage teachers to structure this station to ensure that it is not dominated by teacher-talk but engages the students in active learning. They should not be passive observers; otherwise, the information may as well have been delivered via video. In the following sections, I discuss four strategies you can use to structure this synchronous small-group time: (1) hook the group, (2) I do, we do, groups do, you do, (3) real-time feedback, and (4) present-pause-discuss (repeat).

Strategy 1: Hook the Group

This strategy for structuring the teacher-led station inverts the traditional approach to instruction, which frontloads the process with a clear explanation. Instead, teachers can try shifting the explanation and modeling to the final step of the process. Instead of beginning by presenting information, explaining concepts, or modeling a process, the teacher presents the group with an unfamiliar problem, task, question, or challenge.

Students may need anywhere from five to fifteen minutes, depending on the complexity of the task or problem, to work in pairs or as a group to think critically, communicate, and collaborate in an attempt to solve the problem, complete the task or challenge, or answer the question. This requires that students sit in a space of *productive struggle*, or what Barbara Blackburn (2018), author of multiple books on rigor, calls the sweet spot between scaffolds and support. Instead of jumping in right away to help students when they show signs of needing support, teachers can let them stretch themselves a bit (Blackburn, 2018). In fact, obstacles are an opportunity for them to learn more effectively (Grafwallner, 2021). They must think about what strategies they have used in the past that might work, and lean on their peers as valuable resources. If students are learning online, you can pair them up or create smaller groups of three students and put them in breakout rooms for these conversations.

As students engage in conversation and creative problem solving, the teacher should listen and observe to understand the strategies students are using, identify the gaps in knowledge or skills, and note misconceptions that need addressing. These informal data can help the teacher provide the necessary instruction, supports, and models.

Once the students have had time to work together to try to solve the problem, answer the question, or tackle the task, the teacher pulls them back together to debrief. What strategies did they use? What questions do they have?

The last step in the hook the group structure is the instruction and modeling. It is fascinating to observe how much more interested students are in the explanation once they have sat in a space of productive struggle. Not only does this approach serve to pique students' interest, but over time, it gets them more comfortable approaching unfamiliar problems or tasks. They gain confidence by drawing on their past experiences and collaborating with their peers to engage in creative problem solving.

Figure 4.3 provides a planning template that you can use to implement this strategy.

Target standard:		
Lesson objective or learning goal:		
Lesson elements	**Description of activity**	**How will you differentiate the experience for different groups?**
Hook strategy: Unfamiliar problem, prompt, task, challenge, or question		
Debrief: Discuss strategies applied; review areas of confusion.		
Instruction or modeling: Provide instruction or modeling related to the hook strategy.		
Guided practice: Strategically pair or group students for guided practice.		

FIGURE 4.3: Hook the group strategy-planning template.

*Visit **go.SolutionTree.com/technology** for a free reproducible version of this figure.*

Teachers can differentiate the learning experience in a hook the group format by strategically pairing or grouping students and presenting groups with problems, questions, tasks, or challenges at different levels of academic rigor.

Strategy 2: I Do, We Do, Groups Do, You Do

I do, we do, you do is another name for the direct instruction model (Kilbane & Milman, 2014; Pearson & Gallagher, 1983). I've modified this strategy by adding the *groups do* step to more gradually release the learning to the students and provide you with time to listen and observe students at work, an approach well supported by research (Fisher & Frey, 2014). This additional step allows you to identify which students are ready for individual practice, or the *you do*, and which students would benefit from additional instruction, support, and guided practice with you. This strategy is perfect for introducing a concept, strategy, skill, or process in which students will benefit from both teacher and peer support to understand and implement.

Teachers begin with the *I do*, providing an explanation and a clear model. These modeling sessions are best when teachers make their thinking explicit with a think-aloud.

Once students have had the opportunity to hear a clear explanation and watch the teacher conduct a think-aloud while modeling a strategy, skill, or process, the teacher engages the group in a *we do*. This is an opportunity for the teacher to guide the students through another example or similar task. The teacher can ask students to help solve a similar problem or apply a strategy or skill. During the *we do*, the teacher can gently correct errors, provide feedback, ask follow-up questions, and guide students through the process.

Next comes the *groups do*, an addition to the classic *I do, we do, you do* that allows for a gradual release of responsibility to the learner (Walkup & Squire, 2020). During the *groups do*, the teacher presents groups of students with another similar example or task to work on with peer support, which provides a gradual transition to individual practice. The teacher may want to create mixed skill-level groups to ensure diversity of skills and abilities, allowing stronger students to support students who may need more help. This allows proficient students to strengthen their understanding by explaining key ideas or modeling specific skills for peers who need more support. Alternatively, teachers can group students by their readiness and present groups with examples, problems, or prompts at different levels of academic rigor and complexity. That way, each group is working on a task at a level that will challenge it.

While groups navigate the *groups do* task in the classroom or breakout rooms online, the teacher should focus on listening and observing to collect informal data. This is not a time for the teacher to intervene. It's critical that students have time to engage in productive struggle, attempting the task with peer support to see if they are ready for individual practice. The teacher should notice the strategies students are using and the questions they are asking, and identify the students who seem confused or unsure. The students who are struggling during the *groups do* will need a teacher-led session before transitioning to the *you do* task for independent practice.

Teachers can pull groups together for a quick debrief in which they consider the following questions.

- How did they approach the task?
- What questions do they have?
- Was there anything they were confused about or unsure of?

This allows the students to share what they did, and learn from each other. It also provides the teacher with a clear sense of whether students are ready to transition to the *you do*.

Finally, in the *you do* activity, the students practice without a teacher or peer support. This can be done synchronously, either in class or online. I encourage teachers working online to build a buffer of time into their online sessions to allow students to begin the *you do* task. That way, if they get stuck or hit a bump, they still have access to the teacher to ask a question or seek support.

The planning template in figure 4.4 is a useful way to guide implementation of this strategy.

Target standard:		
Lesson objective or learning goal:		
Lesson elements	Description of activity	How will you differentiate the experience for different groups?
I do: Begin with instruction and modeling.		
We do: Guide the group through an example and ask students to share their ideas.		
Groups do: Group students to continue working with peer support.		
You do: Release students who are ready to independent practice.		

FIGURE 4.4: I do, we do, groups do, you do strategy-planning template.

*Visit **go.SolutionTree.com/technology** for a free reproducible version of this figure.*

Strategy 3: Real-Time Feedback

So often, the focus in the classroom is on transferring information instead of supporting the learning process. Teachers dedicate significant time to explaining concepts, processes, and strategies, but they do not dedicate equal time to supporting implementation. When students take a concept, strategy, or skill and actually attempt to do something with it, that is usually the moment when they get stuck or need help. If we do not prioritize our role supporting learners as they work, students can get frustrated and disengage.

At a real-time feedback station, the teacher dedicates the lion's share of the time to providing students with feedback *as* they work. The teacher might, for example, physically carousel around a small group to look at student work on paper and provide verbal feedback or written suggestions on sticky notes. If students are working online, teachers can jump in and out of digital documents, providing recommendations, asking questions, making suggestions, and linking to additional resources (such as video tutorials). The goal is to support and not to overwhelm with feedback. It is much easier for students to act on focused feedback that targets a specific aspect of their work.

This approach to feedback places value on the process and helps students feel seen and supported as they work. Instead of waiting until an assignment is complete to find out if they did the work correctly, giving focused and actionable feedback as students work will improve the quality of the final product (Hattie & Timperley, 2007; Wisniewski, Zierer, & Hattie, 2020). This approach to feedback has the added benefit of reducing the volume of work teachers take home to provide feedback outside of school hours. Figure 4.5 (page 92) is a real-time feedback planning document designed to help you prepare for these sessions.

Strategy 4: Present-Pause-Discuss (Repeat)

Many teachers may feel like they need to dedicate time to presenting information live so they can customize that explanation for specific groups of learners. Suppose a teacher wants to use the teacher-led station to transfer information. In that case, my suggestion is to break it up and make it as interactive as possible by using a present-pause-discuss (repeat) strategy. This encourages the teacher to chunk the presentation of new information into bite-sized pieces. I recommend that teachers limit the presentation of new information to five-minute chunks to avoid overwhelming students with too much new information at one time.

After presenting each chunk of new information, the teacher pauses, allowing time for students to process the new information and fill in their notes. They may be taking notes on paper using a guided note template or filling in a concept map. Alternatively, teachers may engage groups of learners on a shared digital document to crowdsource notes.

Target standard:
Lesson objective or learning goal:
Feedback focus: What element or elements will you focus on for this feedback session?
Student focus: What will students be working on as they receive feedback?
Expectation for action: What do you want students to do with the feedback?
Time: How much time will you have to give each student feedback?
Format of feedback: Will you provide verbal, written, video, or audio feedback?

FIGURE 4.5: Real-time feedback planning document.

*Visit **go.SolutionTree.com/technology** for a free reproducible version of this figure.*

After giving students time to think about the information the teacher has presented, fill in their notes, and identify any questions they have about the information, the teacher uses the questions generated by the group to facilitate an informal discussion. The goal is to make sure students understand the information before the teacher repeats the process, introducing another chunk of new information. The template shown in figure 4.6 acts as a guide to planning this strategy.

There are myriad ways to structure a teacher-led station that are dynamic, engaging, and differentiated. Teachers may want to use the concept attainment model, and ask students to examine examples and non-examples to learn about a concept. The *concept attainment model* shifts from starting with a definition and explanation followed by examples to beginning with examples that challenge learners to analyze those examples to identify critical attributes or characteristics of a concept. This process positions the leaners as active agents and requires critical thinking. It also benefits from peer-to-peer discussion and collaboration. Teachers can use non-examples to help students contrast what they are noticing about the examples with the non-examples. Teachers will want to nudge deeper thinking during this process by asking open-ended questions. Once students have had the time to discuss their observations,

Target standard:		
Lesson objective or learning goal:		
Lesson elements	**Description of activity**	**How will you differentiate the experience for different groups?**
Present: Chunk the presentation to avoid talking for more than five minutes at a time.		
Pause: Give students time to catch up on their notes or fill in a graphic organizer and collect their thoughts.		
Discuss: Invite students to ask questions about the content and facilitate an informal discussion.		
Repeat: Introduce the next chunk of information and repeat the process as needed.		

FIGURE 4.6: Present-pause-discuss (repeat) strategy-planning template.

*Visit **go.SolutionTree.com/technology** for a free reproducible version of this figure.*

they work collaboratively to craft a definition for the concept that incorporates the critical characteristics or attributes they observed in the examples. Then the teacher follows with explicit instruction to ensure students have an accurate understanding of the concept (Bruner, Goodnow, & Austin, 1956; Kilbane & Milman, 2014; Sukardjo & Salam, 2020). They can facilitate an assignment check and review session in which students use an answer key to check the accuracy of their work, make the necessary corrections, and capture their questions. Teachers may want to begin with a quick assessment to identify the areas of strength and weakness of each group, then provide targeted instruction, reteaching, modeling, and scaffolds to meet the needs of that specific group.

Wrap-Up and Next Steps

As teachers plan instruction for blended learning or online learning environments, they must evaluate the purpose of that time with students and decide which mode of instruction—asynchronous with video or synchronous differentiated small-group instruction—will be the best fit. If teachers are planning to provide the same instruction for all students without modification or differentiation, then recording a video shifts control over the experience to learners. They can pause, rewind, and rewatch videos, making it easier to process and understand that new information. By contrast, teachers who want to differentiate their instruction, guide practice and application, engage students in interactive modeling sessions, facilitate small-group discussions, or provide real-time feedback should prioritize those activities during their synchronous time with students in class as part of a station rotation or online in a video-conferencing session.

Regardless of the mode of instruction, it is crucial to position students as active agents in the learning process. If they are watching a video, we need to encourage them to think critically about that information, and do something meaningful with it. If teachers provide live instruction, they need to create space for students to interact with each other, problem solve, and ask questions.

Teachers' classic role as the instructor has emphasized their content-area or pedagogical expertise. Yet, the more time teachers spend talking, the less time students get to engage with information and each other. Strategically shifting some explanations online with video can create more time and space for teachers to use instructional time and energy to connect with and support individual and small groups of learners.

Along with the reflection questions, consider this next step to further what you've learned in this chapter: select a concept, process, strategy, or skill, and walk through the three-part process of creating a video that incorporates the four recommendations I describe in this chapter for making strong video content. Once you've put your presentation together, choose a screen recording tool and record your video. Then use the three-part flipped lesson template in chapter 3 (page 67) to build a blended lesson around your video instruction. Share your video and three-part lesson with a colleague for feedback, or use it with your students and ask them for feedback.

Chapter 4: Teachers as Instructors and Connectors—Reflect and Discuss

I encourage you to pause here to reflect on or discuss the following questions. If you are reading this book on your own, you can reflect on these questions in a blog post, publish your thoughts on your favorite social media platform, or capture your thoughts in a journal or notebook. If you are reading this book as part of a book club or book study, use the following questions to facilitate vibrant in-person or online discussions.

1. How have you used video with students? How have you used the time created by video instruction? Did it allow you to spend more time working directly with learners?

2. What do you think are the benefits and drawbacks of asynchronous video instruction? How might the approach to creating videos I describe in this chapter mitigate or eliminate some of those challenges?

3. Consider your grade level and content area. What concepts, processes, strategies, or skills do you think you could best capture in a video because all students need to hear these explanations? What concepts, processes, strategies, or skills do you find yourself re-explaining or reteaching throughout the year? If you created videos on those topics that you find yourself repeating each year, how might that positively impact you and your students? Create a list of topics that might make for strong video content.

4. How often do you use whole-group versus small-group instruction? What are the benefits and challenges you associate with each? How might using the station rotation model help you to build more small-group instruction into your lessons?

5. How do you typically structure your live instruction? Is there a balance between teacher-talk and student contributions? How do you engage your students during these live instruction sessions?

6. Which of the four suggestions for structuring live instruction—(a) hook the group; (b) I do, we do, groups do, you do; (c) real-time feedback; or (d) present-pause-discuss (repeat)—was most appealing to you? How can you see yourself using this strategy to structure your teacher-led station? Do you currently differentiate instruction, models, supports and scaffolds, or the level of academic rigor and complexity of application and practice? If so, what strategies do you use?

CHAPTER 5

TEACHERS AS FACILITATORS OF AND PARTNERS IN LEARNING

In a training session with close to 150 educators, I asked the question, "Which role do you spend the most time and energy in?" They had three choices: (1) designer, (2) instructor, or (3) facilitator. They could only choose one of the three options. Ninety-seven participants selected instructor, forty-eight chose designer, and three people selected facilitator. Although I was not shocked by the distribution of responses, it reinforced my belief that teachers need to consider how technology is transforming their value and, by extension, their role in a classroom.

Information is everywhere. We live in a digital age where anyone with a device and an internet connection can access information. A quick online search gives us access to articles, videos, podcasts, interactive websites, and virtual tours that can help us learn anything we want. As a result, technology *should* be radically transforming a teacher's role in the classroom—from content-area experts, as discussed in the previous chapter, to facilitators, which I discuss in this one. Teachers don't need to be experts on everything. We don't need to fear not having the answer. Instead, we can focus our energy on the human side of teaching. This is where our real value lies in a world saturated with technology.

The influx of digital resources and technology tools combined with the changes brought on by the COVID-19 pandemic do demand more from teachers in terms of their design work. Instead of simply following the teacher's edition of a textbook and engaging students primarily offline with pen and paper, teachers are using a variety of online resources to supplement traditional texts and collaborative online work spaces, like Google Workspace (https://workspace.google.com) and Microsoft 365 (https://www.microsoft.com/education/products/office), to assign and collect digital work.

As a result, designing for a blended learning experience demands a higher level of intentionality (Tucker, 2020b).

As you consider how to allocate your finite time and energy resources, it's important to question whether your time is best spent talking at students and transferring information or sitting alongside them guiding them as they wrestle with new information, practice, apply their knowledge, engage in conversations, and attempt to transfer their understanding to new situations. I want educators to leverage technology to make *more* time to connect with learners and support them on their individual learning journeys. I want teachers to design student-centered lessons and learning experiences that free them from the front of the room and allow them to sit with learners and support them as they work. That is the power and potential of blended learning.

> Teachers don't need to be experts on everything. We don't need to fear not having the answer. Instead, we can focus our energy on the human side of teaching. This is where our real value lies in a world saturated with technology.

In this chapter, we will explore five important areas where teachers must invest their time to facilitate learning in a blended learning environment.

1. Partnering with students

2. Supporting metacognitive skill building

3. Facilitating academic discussions in class and online

4. Providing timely, focused, actionable feedback

5. Conferencing one on one with students

Our work in each of these five areas allows us to connect with learners and act as academic coaches to support their growth and development as students *and* people. Blended learning models can make spending time in our role as facilitators doable and sustainable.

Teachers as Partners

A partnership between the teacher and the learner is critical in a blended learning environment where students are active agents who enjoy more control over and assume more responsibility for their learning. Students need motivation to lean into the process of making meaning. They are more likely to do the hard work required of them in classrooms if they view themselves as partners in learning with autonomy and agency in the classroom (Tucker, 2020a). For this to happen, it is critical that we form a meaningful partnership with learners. Some important principles that must underpin this partnership include the following (Tucker, 2020a).

- **Mutual trust and respect:** Establishing mutual respect and trust begins at the start of a school year by prioritizing relationships. Teachers can work with students to co-create class agreements and engage in community-building activities. However, policies around accepting late work or grading can function to either reinforce or erode mutual trust and respect, so it's important to consider the impact of these policies on student partnerships.

- **Shared purpose and goal setting:** It's important for teachers to clearly state the purpose and value of the work they are asking students to do. That way, students understand why they are being asked to engage with a particular task. Goal setting also positions the students to identify academic, personal, and behavior goals that are meaningful to them. This can positively impact their motivation as they begin to see how their behaviors and actions align (or don't) with goals they care about (Ryan & Deci, 2019).

- **Open and honest communication:** Communication cannot flow one way from teacher to learner. Students must have a voice in the classroom with opportunities to talk to the teacher and to one another.

- **Timely, actionable feedback:** Feedback helps students feel seen and supported as they work through a process. Teachers must prioritize feedback in the classroom so students can act on that feedback, ask questions, and seek additional support.

- **A balance of power:** Teachers can share the power in a classroom by giving students more autonomy to work at their own pace and the agency to make key decisions about their learning. At its core, blended learning is a shift in control (or power) from teacher to learner with the goal of working together to ensure each student is making progress toward learning objectives.

- **A shared commitment to learning:** The more willing teachers are to experiment, take risks, fail, and ask for feedback, the more likely students are to feel comfortable doing the same.

These principles highlight critical aspects of our work that we must prioritize and nurture when working with students. Teachers should ask, "How am I proactively developing these principles in my classroom?" This extends far beyond the beginning-of-the-year icebreaker activities and must permeate all aspects of our interactions with learners as well as our approach to expectations, norms, late work, grading policies, and so on. Every decision we make functions to either support or erode these principles.

> A partnership between the teacher and the learner is critical in a blended learning environment where students are active agents who enjoy more control over and assume more responsibility for their learning.

Let's consider the impact that grading practices have on a partnership. Teacher A gives a grade or assigns a point value to every assignment because he believes that without giving a grade, students will not do the work. Teacher A allocates points to students who bring materials to class, complete the assigned review and practice, and participate in class activities, like discussion. He spends a significant amount of his time outside of class grading and entering grades. As a result, he does not have the time or energy to allow his students to revise and resubmit work. When approached by a student who is unhappy with a grade she earned on an assignment and asks about the possibility of spending time on a revision, Teacher A explains that he cannot allow every student to revise and resubmit work because there is no way he can regrade everything. He believes that by grading everything and entering those grades into his online gradebook, he is, in fact, providing both students and parents with timely feedback on their progress.

So, what is the impact of Teacher A's approach to grading on his students? Instead of nurturing a growth mindset where students feel their intelligence and abilities can grow and develop through hard work and practice, it signals that learning has an end point (Dweck, 2015). Students are in a powerless position in this scenario. Despite the desire to continue working and improving, they do not have the opportunity to do so. They might become frustrated or disillusioned in a class where they do not enjoy agency in relation to their grades. Grades in Teacher A's class are something that happens *to* students. If the students in this class have no control over their grades, why should they work hard or take risks? Risks become scary in a classroom where students have just one opportunity to get the right answer or perform well on a specific task.

Now, let's explore Teacher B's approach to grading. Teacher B has decided to limit what she grades to ensure that grades reflect student mastery of specific grade-level concepts and skills. When students practice or review to work with a new idea, concept, skill, or strategy, she does not collect those review and practice assignments to grade. Instead, she provides learners with an answer key or a strong example of the assignment and a simple rubric. She strategically pairs or groups students to work collaboratively to assess their own work. If they have an answer key to check mathematics problems or grammar review, they compare their answers to the key. If they missed a problem, the group members work together to see if they can discover their error and correct it. If they are unsuccessful, they circle that question and seek teacher support. Teacher B believes this self-assessment practice will help learners think critically about their own work, develop their creative problem-solving skills, use peers as resources, and understand their areas of strength and weakness.

If Teacher B's students are working on a piece of writing or a project that spans several days or weeks, her focus is on giving timely, actionable feedback *as* they work. She believes that this feedback shifts the focus to the process and provides learners with the support they need to grow and develop. She does not assign points for completing the various steps of an assignment.

If students have completed an assessment or finished a project, then Teacher B assesses this work with a standards-aligned rubric. She will use a playlist, choice board, or a 5E student-led inquiry to give herself time to assess students' work with them sitting next to her, one by one. (See chapter 7, page 147, to learn more about this model.) During these side-by-side assessments, she conducts a think-aloud as she assesses their work, making her thinking explicit to the student, and she circles the language on the rubric so students understand why they are getting specific scores (Tucker, 2020a). This approach to grading is something Teacher B does *with* and *for* her students. If students are unhappy with their assessment scores or want to spend more time on the piece to improve it, Teacher B allows them the opportunity to revise and resubmit within a designated window of time.

Teacher B's approach to grading is more sustainable because she is not putting points on everything a student touches. Her grading practices engage students as partners, provide them with agency, and reinforce a growth mindset.

Giving students space and agency to practice and make mistakes supports learning—and it's critical that students feel safe to risk these mistakes. Grading everything that students do damages their ability to practice and improve (Townsley & Wear, 2020). Teachers also must consider the very purpose of grading. Assessment and grading expert Tom Schimmer (2016) argues that grades cannot be accurate if practice work is graded. Should we measure students' first fumbling attempts at learning a challenging new skill or their practiced, deft demonstrations of mastery at the end of the unit of learning?

As educators, our policies and practices send signals to our students about what we value. It is critical to question whether these policies and practices function to strengthen our partnership with learners or chip away at it. Doing so requires that teachers engage in regular reflection about why they are doing what they are doing and what the impact is of those decisions on students. What beliefs about teaching and learning drive our decision making? Are our policies and practices in line with our values? Do we make decisions to maintain control in the classroom or to share the responsibility for learning with our students?

Metacognitive Skill Building

To be our true partners, students must get comfortable thinking about their thinking and thinking about their learning. The teacher cannot be the only person in a classroom thinking about student learning and progress. That must be a shared task. However, most students are not used to thinking about their learning in an intentional way. They have probably not received the tools before to do this effectively, so teachers in a blended learning environment must carve out time for metacognitive skill building. Remember that in a blended learning environment, students assume more responsibility for their learning because they have more control over key aspects of their learning, such as time, place, pace, and path. This demands that they develop stronger self-regulation skills to succeed (Susanna et al., 2021). Metacognitive skill building via goal setting, self-assessment, and reflection can help students develop a stronger understanding of themselves as learners. They can begin to ask and answer the following questions.

> The teacher cannot be the only person in a classroom thinking about student learning and progress. That must be a shared task.

- "What strategies or resources are available to me?"
- "Where am I noticing growth in my concept knowledge, skills, and abilities?"
- "Where do I need to spend more time developing?"

- "What support might I need from my teacher or my classmates to continue making progress?"

I know *metacognition*—awareness and understanding of one's own thinking—can feel fairly abstract. But it is enormously beneficial to student learning. Part of metacognition is knowing what one does and doesn't know; thinking intentionally about this can actually strengthen neural pathways (Cohen, Opatosky, Savage, Stevens, & Darrah, 2021). I frame metacognitive skill building in three parts to make the process of developing these skills feel concrete and doable. We must incorporate consistent routines and structures (1) before, (2) during, and (3) after a learning cycle to support students in developing these critical skills, as pictured in figure 5.1.

FIGURE 5.1: Metacognitive skill building in three parts.

Before: Goal Setting

Before students embark on a learning cycle, ask them to set one to three goals for themselves. These can be a combination of academic, behavioral, and personal goals. I like to frame goal setting in three parts: (1) Where am I going?, (2) How will I get there?, and (3) How will I know when I've arrived?

Where Am I Going?

This first question encourages learners of all ages to view learning as a journey. Goal setting is the process of paving their own personal paths forward and setting a destination that is meaningful to them. Teachers can use the following questions to help guide students.

- What is it they want to work on or work toward?
- Is the goal specific and realistic given the time period they will be working on it (for example, week, learning cycle, unit, or grading period)?

- What would be a meaningful goal for them to focus their energy on during this learning cycle?
- Why is this goal meaningful or valuable to them?
- How will reaching this goal positively impact their lives?

These goals should come from students, not a computer program. When students play an active role in setting their own goals, it gives them agency and also creates more buy-in as they work toward those goals.

How Will I Get There?

A journey requires planning and intentionality. Most people don't go on a road trip without an itinerary, snacks, and a reliable vehicle. The same intentionality is required of students if they are going to make substantive progress toward their goals. They need to consider what actions and behaviors are likely to take them closer to their goals. Teachers can use the following questions to help support this thought process in students.

- What will they do to pursue these goals?
- What behaviors are likely to take them closer to achieving these objectives or outcomes?
- What actions or choices might make it harder to achieve these goals?
- What might need to change in terms of their current behaviors, actions, or choices to make them more successful?
- What support might they need from their teacher, peers, or parents to make progress toward these goals?

How Will I Know When I've Arrived?

Finally, teachers must challenge students to consider what success might look or feel like so they are motivated to stick with this work even when the road gets rough. The following questions can help shape these considerations.

- Will there be an internal or external marker that signals that they have successfully reached a goal?
- What would they expect to feel when they reach a particular goal?

These questions encourage students to imagine success and function to motivate them as they anticipate the positive consequences associated with reaching their goals.

Setting the Goals

Teachers should model the process of goal setting for learners just like we would model how to solve a problem or write a sentence. It is a skill that must be explicitly taught. If teachers are working with younger students who are setting goals for the first time, they should dedicate a teacher-led station to supporting this process. That way, the teacher can work with small groups of learners, providing a model, differentiating the level of support and scaffolds needed by a particular group, and guiding them as they attempt to write their goals or even recording goals for learners who may not be able to write them.

Secondary teachers may use a welcome task to incorporate goal setting into their classrooms as a regular routine. If teachers begin each class with a ten-minute welcome activity or task, then setting goals and revising goals can be an activity that they prioritize at the start of each week. On Monday, teachers can ask students to articulate one goal they want to work on that week and think about what they will do to make progress toward that goal, as pictured in figure 5.2. Setting a goal at the start of each week can help frame and focus the students' work and energy that week.

Monday: Goal Setting		
Where am I going this week? What goal do I want to work toward (academically, personally, or behaviorally)?	**How will I get there?** What actions and behaviors will help me achieve my goal?	**When will I arrive?** What will success look or feel like?

FIGURE 5.2: Welcome routine goal-setting activity.

*Visit **go.SolutionTree.com/technology** for a free reproducible version of this figure.*

Alternatively, goal setting using an online template could be an individual online activity as part of a whole-group rotation or the first item on a playlist. Regardless of the model we use to create time for goal setting, it is critical to demonstrate that we value goal setting as a practice by dedicating class time to it.

During: Self-Assessment and Monitoring Progress

Given that most teachers have anywhere from thirty to one hundred and sixty students, it isn't realistic to expect them to know where each student is in individual progress toward mastering a specific concept or skill at any given moment. Instead, this must be a shared responsibility between teachers and learners. We must provide learners with the tools and time to think about their work and what it reveals about their progress. This must be an ongoing process supported by classroom routines and structures.

I encourage teachers to dedicate fifteen to twenty-five minutes a week to a self-assessment activity (Baas et al., 2015; Braund & DeLuca, 2018). The goal of self-assessment is to get students looking critically at their work and developing their ability to identify areas of growth as well as those areas where they need to invest more time and energy to improve. This self-assessment can take place once a week as part of a station rotation or a whole-group rotation.

During a self-assessment, students analyze one of their assignments or work samples from the week. It is helpful to provide students with a self-assessment rubric to guide this metacognitive process. For example, elementary teachers can use a four-image emoji scale to have students align their work with a facial expression (such as a big smile or sad face) or hand gesture (such as thumbs up or down) to reflect how they feel about the pieces they are evaluating. Secondary teachers can use a four-part mastery-based scale (for example, 1 = beginning, 2 = developing, 3 = proficient, and 4 = mastery) to get students to place themselves on this continuum based on what they are seeing in their work.

In addition to aligning their work with a particular level of mastery, students must also reflect on what they learned about their skills, either in writing or in a short video recording. Teachers can use the following questions to encourage these reflections.

- What did they notice in their work?
- Were there particular parts of their assignment that were strong?
- Were there aspects of the assignment that they struggled with or remain confused about?
- Do they feel they are making progress on the skill at the heart of this assignment?

These questions should be used to drive a thoughtful reflection, so students begin to understand themselves better as learners and are able to advocate for themselves.

After: Reflection

At the end of the week or a learning cycle, it is important for students to take the time to reflect on their learning. Teachers can use the following questions to encourage these reflections.

- What did they learn in terms of content and skills? What do they understand on a deeper level than before?

- How did they learn this content or develop their proficiency with these skills? What specific processes, tasks, assignments, interactions, or experiences were most helpful to their process of learning?

- What are they still confused about or need more support in relation to?

Teachers can use these questions to guide learners in thinking more deeply about their learning and what works for them as individuals. It also reinforces their awareness that they are, in fact, learning and making progress. Too often, students jump from activity to activity without ever stopping to appreciate the impact of that work on their skill set or level of understanding. The more they see that the work they do yields tangible results, the more likely they are to stay engaged and persevere through moments of struggle.

Our work facilitating metacognitive skill building is critical to nurturing a healthy partnership with learners. It is through the development of these critical life skills that students will be able to share the responsibility of learning with us, their teachers. That heightened awareness about their learning and growth can also cultivate learners who are able to advocate for themselves, raising a flag to alert us to their specific needs as they progress in their learning journeys.

Academic Discussions in Class and Online

Discussions are a cornerstone of a thriving learning community. It is through academic discourse that students work to make meaning in conjunction with their peers. Academic discussions can take many forms in a blended learning environment. They may take place synchronously in small groups in the classroom, or they may be asynchronous video- or text-based discussions online. Regardless of the form discussions take, the benefits of discussion include the following.

- Challenge students to surface their thinking in a clear and cogent way.

- Expose students to different perspectives and points of view.

- Encourage learners to make connections between ideas and ask questions.

- Drive deeper thinking about topics, texts, and issues.

- Develop stronger speaking and listening skills.

- Orient new learning in a larger context.

Perhaps the most exciting part of academic discourse is that it shifts students from being consumers of other people's ideas to producers of their own ideas. It helps them develop a higher level of confidence with approaching complex topics and engaging in productive struggle. We want to cultivate learners with confidence in their ideas and with the skills necessary to share them with an audience.

> Perhaps the most exciting part of academic discourse is that it shifts students from being consumers of other people's ideas to producers of their own ideas

Regardless of the format a discussion takes, the teacher plays an active role in facilitating that conversation to ensure that it is equitable and productive. Figure 5.3 lists some facilitation strategies along with examples of what they might sound like in practice.

Help students recognize moments of agreement or disagreement.	*"It sounds like Sara and Manuel have two different perspectives on this. Does anyone else want to share their thinking?"*
Present follow-up questions to drive deeper thinking.	*"How might Aiden's point relate to . . .?"*
Prompt students to support their statements.	*"That's an interesting statement, Olivia. What details from the article led you to that conclusion?"*
Encourage students to make connections between ideas or concepts.	*"How does Joshua's comment connect to . . .?"*
Identify strong contributions to the conversation and highlight strong discussion strategies students are using.	*"I appreciate Jose's comment that . . . ."* *"Thank you, Aaliyah, for . . . ."*
Invite quieter students to contribute to the conversation.	*"Steph, what are your thoughts about . . .?"*
Be honest about comments that are unclear or off-topic.	*"I'm not sure I understand your point, David. Can you explain that again?"*
Guide the group toward meaning making.	*"Given our conversation, can we agree on . . .?"* *"What conclusions have we reached about . . .?"*

FIGURE 5.3: Facilitation strategies.

Let's explore three strategies teachers can use to structure discussions for learners of different ages in class and online.

1. Teacher-facilitated fishbowl

2. Four-corner conversations

3. Online discussions

Discussion Strategy 1: Teacher-Facilitated Fishbowl

The *fishbowl*, as pictured in figure 5.4, is a classic cooperative learning strategy that can be useful for onboarding younger learners into academic discussions, promoting active listening, and encouraging students to engage in a critical analysis of a discussion in progress. The fishbowl stratey is flexible enough to take place synchronously in a classroom or in an online video-conferencing session (Han & Hamilton, 2021).

FIGURE 5.4: Fishbowl discussion strategy.

Here is how a fishbowl works. The teacher begins by dividing a group of students in two. This can be the entire class or a smaller group. I prefer doing this with smaller groups of eight to ten students to ensure every student has ample opportunities to speak. Then one half of the group forms the inner circle, and the other half of the group creates an outer circle. These can be literal circles, or if you are online, metaphorical. The students in the inner circle engage in the discussion first, while the students in the outer circle will listen, observe, and document their questions, wonderings, and observations. This can take the form of notes or drawings. The goal is for the outer circle to listen and learn from the conversation happening in the inner circle.

Once the students are in their groups and understand what they will be doing, the teacher presents the group with a discussion question, debatable statement, or a problem to discuss for a specific amount of time. Teachers can use the fishbowl format to have students discuss a text they are reading or a video they have watched, engage in a mathematical problem-solving session, or debate a statement associated with a big idea they are exploring. Depending on the age of the students, teachers may ask them to complete some pre-work to prepare for the conversation, like actively reading a text, view a video, or listen to a podcast.

When the time is up and the inner circle ends its conversation, the outer circle has the opportunity to ask questions, share its observations, and make suggestions designed to improve future discussions or problem-solving sessions. Then they switch roles. The students who were listening and observing have the opportunity to engage in a discussion, and the students who engaged in the conversation move to the outer circle to listen and observe.

Tips for Facilitating an Online Fishbowl

1. Display a two-column chart with the names of students who are in each group clearly visible on their screens to avoid confusion.

2. Use an online timer so students know how much time they have for the discussion.

3. Ask the students in the outer circle to mute themselves while the inner circle is engaged in conversation.

4. Provide the outer circle with a guided note template, graphic organizer, or digital document where they can capture their notes, observations, and questions.

The fishbowl format is flexible enough to work in class or online in synchronous video-conferencing sessions. Teachers can facilitate a fishbowl discussion with the entire class in a whole-group rotation or with a smaller group at the teacher-led station as part of a station rotation lesson. The fishbowl format provides a clear structure for learners, which can ease the anxiety associated with engaging in rapid-fire, real-time conversations. It also encourages a high degree of intentionality because each circle—inner and outer—has a clear task. Students are either focused on adding to the discussion in a meaningful way as part of the inner circle or listening to the discussion and thinking critically about what their peers are saying as part of the outer circle.

Discussion Strategy 2: Four-Corner Conversations

A *four-corner conversation* is a small-group, student-led discussion strategy. Teachers can count students off by four randomly or create four mixed-level speaking and listening groups. Then each group goes to one corner of the classroom, arranges chairs in a circle, and engages in a ten-minute conversation. Figure 5.5 provides a diagram of what this might look like. Teachers can begin with a brainstorming session to generate questions for the groups to select from to guide their conversation, provide questions, or ask members of each group to write one question they would like to discuss prior to moving to the four corners of the classroom.

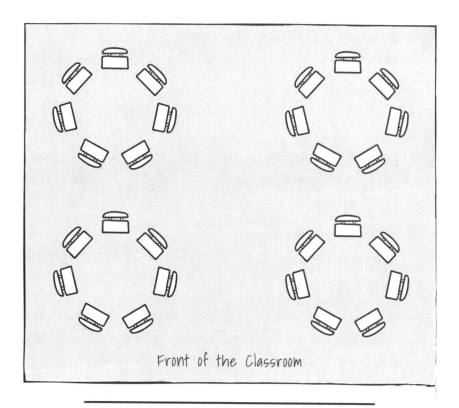

FIGURE 5.5: Four-corner conversations.

The goal of four-corner conversations is for the groups to engage in a student-led conversation about the questions. Depending on the group, teachers may want to ask one student to be the facilitator responsible for guiding the conversation and making sure everyone has an opportunity to speak. Unlike a whole-group discussion, where student responses filter through the teacher, four-corner conversations position the students at the center of the conversation. It is their responsibility to drive the discussion forward with thoughtful comments and questions.

As students engage in discussion, the teacher circulates around the room listening, observing, and considering the following questions.

- What discussion strategies are students using?
- What are they identifying as important points or information?
- Are there any gaps in understanding or misconceptions that the teacher will need to address?
- Are students listening attentively and making eye contact?
- Which students might need additional support either understanding the content they are discussing or engaging more confidently in the conversation?

It is amazing how much a teacher can learn about students by simply watching and listening. In these moments, teachers collect invaluable formative assessment data that they can use to make necessary adjustments to instruction and support.

This strategy is ideal for an offline collaborative task during a whole-group rotation. If students have self-paced through an article, video, or podcast online, they can transition offline to engage in a small-group discussion about what they learned using their peers as resources to understand the information more deeply.

Discussion Strategy 3: Asynchronous Online Discussions

Online discussions are a staple of any online or blended learning course. For years, online discussions were reserved for students with strong enough keyboarding skills to articulate their ideas in writing. However, the emergence of video-based discussion tools, like FlipGrid (https://info.flipgrid.com), has removed that barrier to participating in an online discussion. Now younger learners or students without strong keyboarding skills can also engage in asynchronous video-based discussions.

The biggest benefit of an asynchronous online discussion compared to an in-class discussion is that learners have control over the time, place, and pace of their experience. They can read a question and take time to think about it before crafting a thoughtful reply. Asynchronous online discussions may make engagement more comfortable for students who are shy, need more time to process, or struggle with anxiety. I found that some of my quietest students in the classroom were some of my most outspoken online. Not all students enjoy engaging in the same way. We must create multiple pathways for learners to engage in the class dialogue.

Designing online discussions takes a higher degree of intentionality. Table 5.1 provides an overview of five tips I share with teachers in training sessions to help them craft more engaging discussion questions.

Table 5.1: Five Tips for Designing Dynamic Online Discussion Questions

Tip	Description
Tip 1: Start with a creative and catchy title.	This is how you will hook your students' attention and pull them into the conversation.
Tip 2: Layer your questions to subtly differentiate.	Ask three questions instead of one to allow for multiple entry points into the conversation.
Tip 3: Vary your question types.	Use a variety of question types to keep students engaged over time.
Tip 4: Include media.	Add images, graphics, or video clips to complement your questions, grab your students' attention, and provide additional information about the topic.
Tip 5: Provide directions for student participation.	Clearly explain what students need to do once they have answered the question. How many peers should they respond to? How long should their responses be? Are there any strategies you can suggest they use in their replies to keep them substantive?

Let's explore these tips in more detail. For tip 1, I recommend that teachers use the title of the discussion question to hook their students. We want to grab their attention and pique their interest with our titles. "Chapter 3 discussion question" isn't going to inspire students to dive into the discussion, but titles like "Is love at first sight possible?," "Is graffiti really art?," or "Should junk food be taxed at a higher rate?" might draw them into the conversation more effectively.

For tip 2, I encourage teachers to avoid asking a single question. Instead, ask three questions and allow students to choose the question they feel the most confident answering. Asking a single question only allows for one entry point into the conversation. We are more likely to engage all students if we present multiple questions and provide students the agency to select the question *they* want to answer. Our classes comprise a wide range of skills, abilities, and language proficiencies, so this strategy makes it possible to subtly differentiate within the conversation. Teachers can begin with the most academically rigorous question, and make the subsequent questions more accessible by using simpler vocabulary or even shifting from one question type (see the next tip), like debate or analytical, to a less rigorous question type, like reflection, that allows students to draw on their own life experience.

For example, an upper elementary class might engage in the following online discussion as part of a health or science unit:

> **Title:** *A Tax on Junk Food*
>
> **Questions:** *Why would some members of congress want to add an additional tax to junk food? How does eating junk food negatively impact people specifically and society more generally? How do you think students your age would react to paying more for junk food?*

This next example targets a secondary art class:

> **Title:** *The Intersection of Art and Life*
>
> **Questions:** *How does life, specifically political, social, and/or religious movements manifest in artwork? Why does art often reflect life or the artist's culture? Does the art you enjoy say something about you–your interests, culture, or experiences?*

The third tip is related to the previous tip: be aware of the types of questions you tend to ask and make sure to keep your discussion questions varied. Students enjoy variety, so switching up the types of questions you are asking can keep student interest in online discussions high over time. Some of the question types you might consider using to structure your discussion questions include the following.

- Analytical
- Synthesis
- Compare and contrast
- Cause and effect
- Debate
- Reflection

Some of these question types are more cognitively challenging to answer than others, so keep your students in mind when crafting questions to ensure they are within their abilities to answer them. As demonstrated in both of the sample questions from tip 2, student must first analyze or evaluate a topic, which is more challenging, and the final question asks them for their opinion or to reflect on their life experience.

My fourth tip is that media is a must! We are teaching a generation of visual learners, and they respond to images, graphics, memes, videos, infographics, and so on. Find something visual related to your question and embed it into the question. It is likely to spark more interest in the question. For example, the elementary discussion topic about taxing junk food could include a photo of a fast food meal, an infographic about how much fast food Americans consume in a year, or a video clip from the documentary film *Supersize Me* (Spurlock, 2004). The secondary discussion topic on art could include an image of artwork or a video of a museum tour.

And finally, for tip 5, include explicit directions for what students should do once they have answered your question. How do you want them to engage with their classmates? A discussion isn't simply about providing an answer. It is about engaging with the other members of the learning community, so we must clearly signal that their work is not done when they have submitted their answer. Tell them how many of their classmates you want them to post a reply to and provide some strategies they can use to make those replies substantive. For example, you could include a statement like this:

> After you have posted your response to the question, read the responses posted by your peers and reply thoughtfully to at least two other members of the class. You can make connections, build on ideas shared, respectfully present a different perspective, or ask questions in your reply.

As with any skill, participating in an online discussion takes practice. Students will need explicit instructions about what is expected of them online. I recommend that teachers make facilitating an online discussion sustainable by limiting their own replies to students to the number of replies they expect from a single student. That is, if you have asked students to reply to two classmates, then you should only post replies to two students. This will ensure that you do not overpower the conversation or create too much work for yourself. Let students know what to expect from you in the conversation and use your replies to model strong participation.

> I'd recommend that teachers make facilitating an online discussion sustainable by limiting their own replies to students to the number of replies they expect from a single student.

Discussions among students are critical if they are going to wrestle with complex concepts and construct knowledge as a community. It is also important in a partnership that students have opportunities to engage in one-on-one conversations with their teacher. Conferencing (see page 118) is one way to consistently build time into class for these conversations about student progress.

Timely, Focused, Actionable Feedback

Feedback is how students feel seen and supported in class, online, or a blend of the two. It shifts the focus from products to the process of learning. When students feel that teachers value the process, it creates an incentive to invest more time and energy into their work. Additionally, the more feedback students receive as they work on a task, the more likely they are to grow and develop as learners. Effective feedback is timely, focused, and actionable (Hattie & Timperley, 2007; Wisniewski et al., 2020). Unfortunately, traditional approaches to giving feedback tend to be problematic.

> Feedback is how students feel seen and supported in class, online, or a blend of the two. It shifts the focus from products to the process of learning. When students feel that teachers value the process, it creates an incentive to invest more time and energy into their work.

The first problem with traditional feedback is that teachers often take student work home to give feedback. It is not something they typically do *with* the students in class. So, it makes sense why feedback would not be timely. Teachers have full lives beyond the classroom and should not be expected to spend hours in their evenings or on the weekends leaving comments on student work. Instead, it is critical that teachers employ blended learning models to keep feedback in the classroom so it is timely and sustainable.

Second, traditional feedback often focuses on minutia. When teachers provide traditional feedback, they tend to cover a lot of ground, leaving numerous comments and suggestions. This can be challenging for students to understand, process, and act on. Instead, teachers should, like an athletic coach on the field, identify one aspect of the student's performance and provide feedback on that single element. That way, students can focus on making that specific improvement or adjustment. Instead of feeling overwhelmed by comments, students feel empowered to focus their energy on a single aspect of their work. This will help them develop their confidence in their abilities over time.

Finally, teachers traditionally provide feedback on finished products, so there is no incentive for students to do anything with that feedback. I maintain that feedback on finished products is a waste of teacher time because it is not actionable. If teachers don't ask students to act on feedback to improve their work, then that feedback is unlikely to result in significant improvements. By comparison, when teachers give feedback on work in progress, students can act on it to create a stronger finished product.

When I work with teachers, I ask them to consider this question: How much time do you spend providing instruction (expert) versus supporting students as they work (facilitator)? I believe the ratio of time dedicated to each should, at the least, be equal. We can spend all day telling students how to do something, but it is only when they actually put pencil to paper or fingers to keys that they are likely to hit a bump and need support. That's why our work providing real-time feedback is critical.

I know teachers are under immense pressure to cover a ton of content and curriculum, but it does no good to race through them if students do not actually understand or cannot employ the skills they are learning. Teachers can create videos to shift some instruction online, and use the station rotation model to capture the process of giving feedback in the classroom.

Since teachers have limited time with each group in a station rotation lesson, these feedback sessions at the teacher-led station must be focused out of necessity. Prior to a real-time feedback session, select one aspect of the students' work to focus on. Make your focus explicit to learners so they understand that you are not trying to fix all the errors in their work. You can say something like:

> Today I'll be providing feedback on [insert area of focus]. When I've left a comment or suggestion for you, please use it to improve that aspect of your work. If you have questions as you work, please [insert directions for where students will capture their questions].

That last sentence is important because you won't have a lot of time to give feedback. Learners can unintentionally derail a feedback session when they interrupt your thought process by asking verbal questions. Instead, encourage them to note their questions in a specified location (for example, write them on a sticky note or capture them in a comment on their document).

The beauty of these real-time feedback sessions in a teacher-led station is that students can immediately act on that feedback, making it more effective (Wisniewski et al., 2020). It also means teachers are not taking this work home to provide feedback outside of school hours. Finally, it functions to reinforce our partnership with learners, sending the message that we are in this together, and we care enough about them to dedicate class time to providing them with feedback to help them grow and develop.

One-on-One Conferences With Students

Conferencing takes time, so to accommodate it, teachers will need to design learning experiences that do not require that they direct the lesson. You can use strategies like a playlist, choice board, 5E instructional model (see chapter 7, page 147), choose your learning path adventure, or flipped lesson to create the time and space to meet with individual students for these critical conversations. It's also important to note that they do not all have to happen in a single day or even consecutive days. It may feel more manageable to spread them out and meet with a few students each week.

As students develop their metacognitive muscles, their increased awareness of their skills, progress, and needs can allow them to take a more active role in the classroom. They will also benefit from engaging in conversations with their teacher to discuss their skills, progress, and needs, which is why conferencing is a cornerstone of blended learning. That is why I developed the 4Ps conferencing framework to prioritize student agency in the conferencing process. The goal of the 4Ps conferencing framework— (1) purpose, (2) preparation, (3) post-conference plan, and (4) parent communication—is to ensure that conferencing reinforces the partnership between teacher and learner. Figure 5.6 is a student handout (physical or digital) that teachers can use to help learners work through the framework.

Student Conference			
Pre-conference		During the conference	Post-conference
Purpose	Preparation	Post-conference plan	Parent communication
		Student action items: Teacher action items:	

FIGURE 5.6: The 4Ps conferencing framework.

*Visit **go.SolutionTree.com/technology** for a free reproducible version of this figure.*

Purpose

Purpose positions learners to decide how they want to use this time with the teacher. Do they want to discuss their progress toward goals, performance in the class, or an area of frustration or challenge? Would they prefer to use the time to get feedback on some work in progress or discuss an assignment they struggled with? The goal of the first P is for *students* to decide how best to use this time. What would feel most valuable to them?

Preparation

Preparation requires that students prepare for the conference to ensure the time is as productive as possible. Will they need to bring their goal-setting sheet, a specific piece of work, or questions to this conversation? This part of the framework reinforces the idea that conferencing is the students' time with the teacher and they need to come prepared to maximize that time.

Post-Conference Plan

A *post-conference plan* involves both the student and the teacher capturing notes or action items. These are specific things they will each do to ensure the learner makes progress moving forward. Does the student want additional support in a particular area? Will the teacher provide some individualized instruction or additional feedback? Does the student need to spend more time practicing a skill or working with a concept?

Parent Communication

Parent communication asks learners to share the focus and outcome of the conference with their parents or guardians, usually by passing on a voice memo, email, or glow-and-grow document. A *glow-and-grow document*, which may be more accessible for elementary school learners, is a form that prompts them to share an example of something they are proud of (*glow*—as in glowing with pride) and an example of something they want to continue working on (*grow*—as in an area in need of growth). The goal is for students to begin to own the conversation about their progress and growth. If students are going to be invested in their learning, updating their caregivers about their progress is an important step.

Wrap-Up and Next Steps

In a digital age where information is everywhere, the true value teachers bring to the classroom is their humanity and ability to work alongside students to facilitate learning. This reality must be apparent in the work we do and roles we spend time in. It is our ability to connect with learners and facilitate learning that is likely to have the greatest impact on students. Teachers who proactively form partnerships with learners are more likely to feel successful facilitating learning in a classroom and online. In order for a partnership to be successful, teachers must see students as true and capable collaborators in learning and help them develop the metacognitive skills necessary to think about their learning. Our facilitation work requires that we provide opportunities for the classroom community to engage in academic discourse, prioritize feedback to support students as they work, and offer regular conferencing sessions with students. All of these aspects of our work will function to strengthen our relationships with students and make the work we do more rewarding.

Consider these next steps to further your learning in this chapter. See also the reflection questions.

- Design an online academic discussion question using the tips presented in figure 5.6 (page 118). Make sure to include the following items.
    - ¤ Start with a catchy title intended to hook your students' attention.
    - ¤ Decide what types of question you want to ask (for example, debate, analytical, and compare and contrast).
    - ¤ Layer your questions to offer multiple entry points into the conversation and subtly differentiate for your diverse group of students.
    - ¤ Insert media related to the question to pique student interest.
    - ¤ Include specific guidelines for their interactions with each other.
- Once you have designed your question, create a list of strategies you think can help your students engage with each other in a substantive and meaningful way. Pair those strategies with sentence frames to support students' early interactions with each other.

Chapter 5: Teachers as Facilitators and Partners in Learning—Reflect and Discuss

I encourage you to pause here to reflect on or discuss the following questions. If you are reading this book on your own, you can reflect on these questions in a blog post, publish your thoughts on your favorite social media platform, or capture your thoughts in a journal or notebook. If you are reading this book as part of a book club or book study, use the following questions to facilitate vibrant in-person or online discussions.

1. Imagine you have a pie, and you need to divide it to reflect how much time you spend in each of your three roles: (a) designer, (b) instructor, and (c) facilitator. I encourage you to make this metaphorical pie an actual drawing. Draw a circle on a piece of paper and divide the circle into labeled sections to reflect the percentage of time you currently spend in each role. Label this pie "Now." What do you notice about your pie? Which role are you spending the most time in? Is that a rewarding role? Does it afford you time to connect with individual students to support their progress?

2. Now, draw a second circle and label it "Future Goal." Divide the pie to reflect how you *want* to use your time and energy as you work with the various blended learning models to reimagine your approach to designing learning experiences. How is this future goal pie different from the original? What changes might you need to make to create this new reality? What impact might this division of time and energy have on your feelings of job satisfaction and your relationships with learners?

3. Consider the partnership principles I present in this chapter. Think about one of your policies or practices (for example, grading, late work, or homework). How does that policy or practice function to reinforce a partnership with students or erode it? What beliefs about teaching and learning drive your decision to use that particular policy or practice? If it has the potential to erode your partnership with learners, how might you reimagine it so that it instead reinforces your partnership with students?

4. How much time do you currently dedicate to metacognitive skill building? How might a regular practice of setting goals, tracking and monitoring progress, and reflecting on learning impact your students' behavior and motivation over time? How can you use blended learning models to ensure these activities are sustainable? What supports or scaffolds will your students need to succeed in setting goals, tracking progress, and reflecting on their learning?

5. If you had to compare the amount of time you currently spend on instruction compared to the amount of time you spend giving feedback, what would that ratio look like? How might you adjust your current practice to ensure you are dedicating as much time to feedback as you are to instruction? Which models do you see yourself using to make time for feedback in the classroom? How might a focus on feedback impact your students over time?

6. Which discussion strategy that I present in this chapter is most appealing given the content area and grade level you teach? Why are you drawn to this particular strategy? What support (for example, sentence frames) might students need to successfully engage in a discussion using this strategy?

7. Do you currently conference with learners? If so, how do you structure these conversations? If not, how might using blended learning models create the time and space for these important conversations? What are your thoughts on the 4Ps conferencing framework? What modification might you need to make for your learners?

8. What was your big takeaway from this chapter? What idea resonated with you the most? How might this idea impact the way you approach your work as a teacher in a blended learning environment?

The Complete Guide to Blended Learning © 2022 Solution Tree Press • SolutionTree.com
Visit go.SolutionTree.com/technology to download this free reproducible.

A DYNAMIC LEARNING COMMUNITY

After my first year of teaching, I was pink-slipped along with all the other teachers who, like me, had temporary status. Instead of waiting to see if the school district would rehire me, I applied for a position at another high school, where I would ultimately spend the next fifteen years of my career. From the moment the principal called me to tell me I had the job, my experience at Windsor High School in Sonoma County, California, was different from my first job. Before school started, teachers attended a two-day staff retreat. I remember initially groaning about having to go. It's always a little awkward for me to enter an unfamiliar environment where I don't know anyone. Despite my initial hesitation and anxiety, I had a blast. We played games, engaged in meaningful conversations, shared meals, and got to know one another beyond the surface hellos that had characterized the relationships between the colleagues at my first school.

This early work that the school leadership did to build community and develop relationships among the teaching staff helped me feel safe sharing my ideas in department meetings and asking for help when I needed it. When I walked across campus, people stopped me to chat and ask how I was doing. I felt like I was part of a community, and that feeling is one of the reasons I was content to stay at that school for so many years.

Just as leadership welcomed me into the school community, we must welcome students into our classrooms, and proactively build a learning community to ensure that students fully realize their social presence. The strength of a learning community directly impacts students' ability to engage in the process of meaning making together. The work to develop a dynamic learning community extends beyond a collection of icebreakers during the first week of school. Community is something we cultivate, maintain, and nurture all year long. It's essential that all students feel safe, respected, and supported in our classrooms if they are going to take risks and engage fully (Schmitt, Branscombe, Postmes, & Garcia, 2014; Verkuyten, Thijs, & Gharaei, 2019).

In this chapter, I'll describe the role of the social presence in a blended learning environment and use five components of the Collaborative for Academic, Social, and Emotional Learning (CASEL, n.d.) framework as a lens to organize a collection of strategies to help students develop the skills necessary to thrive in a learning community.

SEL and the Social Presence

To understand the concept of the social presence, it's first necessary to understand the definition and importance of SEL. CASEL (n.d.) defines it as

> the process through which all young people and adults acquire and apply the knowledge, skills, and attitudes to develop healthy identities, manage emotions and achieve personal and collective goals, feel and show empathy for others, establish and maintain supportive relationships, and make responsible and caring decisions.

Given the emphasis on SEL in schools, this chapter directly links the dimensions of SEL, as the CASEL framework describes it, and the cultivation of a social presence in a learning community. The more opportunities you give your students to develop the following five competencies in the CASEL (n.d.) framework, the more likely you are to create a robust social presence in your blended learning environment: (1) relationship skills, (2) self-awareness, (3) social awareness, (4) self-management, and (5) responsible decision-making skills. The competencies are key to establishing equitable and productive learning environments, and they can help teachers develop a social presence in their classrooms, helping students feel safe engaging authentically with their learning, whether that engagement is in person, online, or a blend of the two (CASEL, n.d.).

Thus, the *social presence* is the dimension of the community of inquiry framework that deals with learners' ability to project their social identity in an online or blended learning environment (Kreijns et al., 2014). This expression of social identity and self, both in person and online, is critical to authentic participation in the process of constructing knowledge as part of a learning community (Swan, 2019). Students must view each other as real people with feelings, beliefs, and values, especially when working online where the screen is mediating their interactions and may make exchanges feel less personal. In a blended learning environment, you must intentionally develop this social presence in your classroom and online to ensure students feel connected to and comfortable with one another regardless of the learning landscape.

The social presence comprises three parts: (1) affective expression, or the expression of beliefs, feelings, and values, (2) open and honest communication, and (3) group cohesion. These behaviors are essential to developing a high-functioning learning community (Swan, 2019), and they can be developed by focusing on the five SEL competencies. The teacher's role is central to creating and maintaining a learning environment that invites students to express their social identities, engage respectfully with diverse peers, and work collaboratively to make meaning. Explicitly teaching SEL skills can help students develop a complete understanding of themselves and learn how to engage with others in a kind, empathetic, and responsible way.

The following sections explore how you can develop your blended classroom's social presence through the lens of the five SEL competencies.

Relationship Skills

CASEL (n.d.) defines *relationship skills* as the abilities necessary "to establish and maintain healthy and supportive relationships and to navigate settings with diverse individuals and groups effectively." The quality of relationships among members of a learning community directly impacts how safe students feel taking interpersonal risks, sharing their ideas, engaging in collaborative tasks, and taking academic and social risks. Regular informal conversations, activities like class scavenger hunts, and sharing information about their lives via a random autobiography are all strategies that can help students get to know one another and develop their relationship skills in an education context.

Relationship-Building Strategy 1: Daily Informal Conversations

Begin every class or small-group interaction with an informal check-in or conversation starter. These conversations can happen as a whole group, in small groups, or with a partner.

- **High and low:** Ask students to share a high and a low from the week. About what are they feeling good or confident? What are they struggling with or finding challenging? This exercise reminds students that everyone experiences moments of joy and frustration.

- **Energizing and draining:** Encourage students to reflect on their day or week, and share something in their lives that has been energizing and something that has been draining. This check-in may also provide insight into students' lives that can help you develop empathy for them.

- **A moment of gratitude:** Invite students to identify someone or something in their lives that they are grateful for, and ask them to explain how this person or thing has positively impacted their lives. Cultivating gratitude can ease anxiety, foster a sense of well-being, and help individuals form relationships (Cregg & Cheavens, 2021).

- **Superpower icebreaker:** Ask students to select one superhuman ability that they would like to possess. Why did they choose this power? How would this superhuman ability positively impact their lives?

- **"Would you rather?":** Present students with two options (for example, tacos or pizza or mountains or beach) and ask them to explain their choice.

The goal of these check-ins and icebreakers is to get students comfortable with engaging in conversation, listening actively, sharing their thoughts and feelings with classmates, and feeling heard by others.

Relationship-Building Strategy 2: Class Scavenger Hunt

Scavenger hunts are a fun way to help students learn about each other, appreciate differences, and find points of commonality among class members. You can ask students to submit fun facts about themselves at the start of the school year, and use those to create your scavenger hunts. Alternatively, you can create a more general list of questions, and ask students to find classmates who have a particular characteristic or have had a specific experience. The following list provides some examples.

- "Who went camping this summer?"
- "Who speaks two languages?"
- "Who is left-handed?"
- "Who is a middle child?"
- "Who went swimming in the ocean this summer?"
- "Who owns a reptile?"
- "Who is a vegetarian?"

The goal of a class scavenger hunt is to get students engaging in one-on-one conversations with peers. If they complete the scavenger hunt as a community-building activity at the start of the school year, encourage them to begin these conversations by introducing themselves. Then they can ask a series of questions to learn about one another and attempt to fill in items on their scavenger hunt sheet. You can limit them to using a single student's name one time to encourage them to meet as many classmates as possible in the time allowed.

Relationship-Building Strategy 3: Random Autobiography

If you have ever started the school year by asking your students to write you a letter of introduction, you know they can be bland and don't provide much insight into your new students. I learned about the random autobiography format as an alternative to the classic welcome letter in graduate school. It is essentially a free verse poem composed of lines that reveal random facts about the student's life. You should provide students with a collection of sentence starters to support them as they compose their random autobiographies, such as in figure 6.1 (page 130).

The beauty of this assignment is that students share quirky details about themselves that help you connect with them more quickly at the start of the year. Instead of requiring that they share their entire random autobiography with the class, you can ask them to identify a few lines they don't mind sharing. Then, you can begin a series of lessons by asking students to share a line with the group to build community and help them get to know one another.

You will get better results if you write and share your random autobiography with students as a vehicle to introduce yourself to them and to model the purpose and value of the assignment. Students are usually curious about their teachers, and this assignment can make you more relatable and less intimidating at the beginning of the year.

Self-Awareness

CASEL (n.d.) defines *self-awareness* as the ability to "understand one's own emotions, thoughts, and values and how they influence behavior." To project their social identities in a learning environment, students must understand themselves as people and learners, which is another reason metacognitive skill building is critical. They need to practice identifying their emotions, linking their feelings to their behaviors, and reflecting on their strengths and weaknesses. Students with high levels of self-awareness have a strong sense of purpose and a growth mindset; they understand that their intellect and skills are not fixed but can be developed through hard work and practice (Dweck, 2015). Regular check-ins about feelings, activities designed to get them exploring their identities, and practicing mindful breathing can positively impact a learner's ability to engage with other members of the learning community positively and productively.

I was born in (season, month) . . .

I am told that I . . .

I love (or loved) to . . .

I've held a . . .

I remember . . .

I've heard . . .

I believe . . .

I used to . . .

I cannot believe that I . . .

I enjoy . . .

I avoid . . .

I have learned that . . .

In my free time, I love to . . .

When people describe me, they say I'm . . .

I remember how it felt to . . .

FIGURE 6.1: Random autobiography sentence starters.

*Visit **go.SolutionTree.com/technology** for a free reproducible version of this figure.*

Self-Awareness Strategy 1: Check-Ins About How Students Are Feeling

Conversations about feelings are often absent in classrooms, but students' emotions (especially negative ones like anxiety, fear, and sadness) directly impact their ability to focus and engage in a learning experience (Stasiak, 2017). Taking a moment to ask students to think about and articulate their emotional state is one way to help them develop self-awareness over time. Students need to understand how they are feeling to know why they are responding to a teacher, classmate, or situation in a particular way (Cohen et al., 2021; Vago & Silbersweig, 2012).

Following is a collection of check-in prompts that teachers can use to engage students in a verbal sharing session or a written reflection about their feelings in a particular moment.

- **Two words:** Brené Brown (2010), a researcher and author whose TED Talk on vulnerability is one of the most viewed of all time, starts her meetings by inviting her team members to share two words that reflect how they are feeling at that moment (Schawbel, 2013). The goal is to create space for these feelings and allow people to feel seen (Mikel, 2020). You can begin your class this way by going around the room and having students check in verbally. You can also ask them to do a quick write in which they identify their two words and explain why they chose those words.

- **Emoji mood meter:** Allow students to identify or describe the emoji that best reflects their feelings or mood in a given moment. Why did they select this particular emoji? How does this face or object reflect their current mood or state of mind?

- **Song of the day:** Challenge students to select a song that represents how they are feeling. What about this song matches their current mood: tempo, lyrics, volume, or instruments? Ask them to explain their choice.

Self-Awareness Strategy 2: Exploring Identity

Project Zero (2019d) from Harvard's Graduate School of Education has developed a thinking routine titled "Who Am I?" that encourages students to reflect deeply about themselves and their identity while "developing a greater understanding of similarities and differences" within a diverse class community.

You can ask your students to complete their responses in writing or a visual art format (for example, drawings or collages), or you could create a digital slide deck with a slide for each student, as pictured in figure 6.2. One advantage of a digital slide deck is that it ensures visibility, allowing students to explore one another's slides to learn about the other members of the class community.

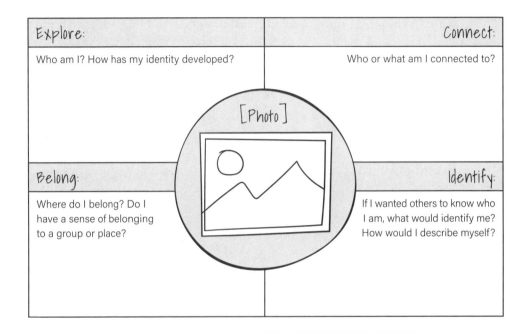

FIGURE 6.2: "Who Am I?" thinking routine sample slide.

Self-Awareness Strategy 3: Practice Mindful Breathing

Research has shown that mindful breathing reduces stress and anxiety, decreases negative thoughts, and improves feelings of well-being (Bazzano, Anderson, Hylton, & Gustat, 2018; Van de Weijer-Bergsma, Langenberg, Brandsma, Oort, & Bögels, 2012). In the rush of their day-to-day schedules, students may not have time to engage in a mindfulness activity. Yet, the simple act of closing the eyes, focusing on breathing, and releasing negative thoughts can immediately and positively impact the body. Teachers can help students ground and center themselves by building in opportunities for short breathing exercises or guided meditations at the start of class, before a collaborative task, or ahead of any type of performance task or assessment.

Following up a mindful breathing exercise with a short check-in with a partner or quick write can also help students appreciate the impact of the experience. Questions they can use as prompts include the following.

- How did they feel when they entered the classroom? Were they anxious, tired, worried, or frustrated?

- How are they feeling after taking a few minutes to close their eyes and focus on breathing? Do they feel more relaxed, calm, or centered?

- Was there any thought, in particular, that was hard to release during the exercise?

Social Awareness

CASEL (n.d.) defines *social awareness* as the ability to "understand the perspectives of and empathize with others, including those from diverse backgrounds, cultures, and contexts." Social awareness requires that students recognize social norms and behaviors appropriate for different contexts, take the perspective of other individuals—that is, assume their point of view, appreciate differences, and empathize with others. Given the anonymity most students associate with a screen and online interactions, it's essential to develop social awareness so students act in a socially responsible way, both in person and in an online setting. Taking time to co-create class agreements, engage in role-playing activities, and establish appropriate consequences can help strengthen our students' social awareness.

Social-Awareness Strategy 1: Co-Create Class Agreements

It's common for teachers to give students rules at the start of the school year, but students typically have no ownership over those rules and are less likely to feel compelled to comply with them. However, in a blended learning environment, the goal is to shift more control over the learning experience to students. Allowing the students to drive the decision making about what norms and expectations would make their time together feel safe, supportive, and productive shifts the responsibility for thinking about expectations for behavior from teacher to learner.

Start by asking students to take a few minutes to reflect on their experiences in school and identify one moment when they felt welcomed, accepted, and supported by classmates and one moment when their feelings were hurt, or classmates made them feel sad, angry, hurt, or unsafe. What did their classmates do that made them feel good? What did their classmates do that made them feel bad? You can ask them to capture their examples in drawings or words.

Once students have had time to reflect on their past experiences, put them in small groups and ask them to share their positive and negative experiences. This share-out reminds students that everyone has experienced both positive and negative situations in school. They can work collaboratively to identify behaviors and norms that they believe will lead to productive and positive interactions in class and online. They may highlight behaviors like *use each other's names* or *respectfully disagree if you have a different perspective.*

After identifying the positive behaviors they want to encourage in the classroom and online, they can identify those behaviors they believe could harm the class community. What might make people feel uncomfortable with sharing their ideas or opinions, asking questions, or taking risks? They may highlight behaviors like *don't attack the person when you disagree with an idea* or *don't type a response if you are angry.*

You can provide each group with a two-column chart to capture their dos and don'ts for behavior. Once each group has had time to complete their list of dos and don'ts, pull the class together to identify the areas of overlap between the various lists, and compile a class list. You can ask students to review the final draft and sign it to acknowledge their intention to follow the established list of expected behaviors.

Social-Awareness Strategy 2: Practice Perspective Taking

Taking another person's perspective—attempting to view a situation through the eyes of someone else—is key to having empathy. You can engage your students in role-playing activities to encourage them to step into someone else's shoes for a moment and consider how that person might be feeling in a particular situation. You can present your students with everyday scenarios that students their age face in classrooms, on school campuses, or online. Following are a few example scenarios.

- **Scenario 1:** A student enters the room and sees a few friends huddled together, talking and laughing. As the student approaches, the group becomes silent and breaks apart.

- **Scenario 2:** After a student posts a picture online, another student makes a sarcastic comment about the first student's clothing.

- **Scenario 3:** In a group assignment, one student takes charge, giving orders to the other two students in the group.

Alternatively, you can break students into groups and ask *them* to generate scenarios that students their age encounter that are challenging or uncomfortable. Then they can exchange scenarios with another group and engage in a role-playing exercise. After each role-playing exercise, the group should pause to discuss what people in the situation might think or feel. What motivates their behavior? How does their behavior impact the other people in the scene? Asking students to imagine what it is like to be another person can help remind them how their actions may intentionally or unintentionally impact other people.

Social-Awareness Strategy 3: Decide on Appropriate Consequences for Missteps

Missteps in the classroom and online can happen to anyone. Learning how to navigate different learning environments and contexts requires practice. It is vital to have a clear set of consequences in place to deal with these missteps. Just as allowing students to co-create the expectations for behavior gives them ownership over that process, it is similarly valuable to position learners at the center of the conversation about consequences. If someone violates the don'ts that the class agreements articulate, what is an appropriate response or consequence? Allow students the time and space to engage in conversation and capture their thinking in drawings or words. Then pull the class together to debrief, and compile their ideas into a single list of consequences. You may want to create a document with these consequences clearly articulated, and send a copy home for parents and guardians to review and sign so that everyone is on the same page about the class's established behavioral expectations and the consequences of not following them.

Self-Management

CASEL (n.d.) defines *self-management* as the ability "to manage one's emotions, thoughts, and behaviors effectively in different situations and to achieve goals and aspirations." Self-management encompasses students' ability to set goals and work toward those goals, self-regulate and manage their emotions and stress in a healthy way, and employ organizational strategies and skills to manage their workload. In addition to the strategies I discuss in the following subsections, you may want to incorporate routines designed to help students hone their organization skills. You can show them how to organize a traditional or digital notebook, use an online calendar to track assignments, and set reminders to help them stay on top of their workload.

Creating a vision board, setting short-term goals, and offering a mood-management choice board can help students successfully manage their emotions and behaviors to thrive in a blended learning environment.

Self-Management Strategy 1: Create a Vision Board

A *vision board* is a visual representation of hopes, dreams, and goals, as pictured in figure 6.3 (page 136). It is also a great way to learn more about your students. When you articulate the why or value of a vision board for your students, explain that research shows the mental practice of visualizing positively impacts motivation and self-directed learning (Hematian, Rezaei, & Mohammadyfar, 2017).

FIGURE 6.3: Example of a vision board.

Once you've articulated the purpose of a vision board, guide them through the following two steps to help them create a vision board that is meaningful and motivating.

1. **Time to reflect:** Just as you ask students to complete a prewriting or brainstorming activity to generate ideas for a writing assignment, it's essential to give them time to reflect on what is important to them personally and academically in advance of creating their vision boards. Encourage them to generate a list of words or create rough sketches to capture their thinking about specific goals they have for themselves this school year.

2. **Select a medium:** Students who prefer a tactile, offline experience can create a vision board on poster paper by sketching their images or creating a collage from old magazines. Students who enjoy working online can create their collages using an online program or digital document. Giving students the agency to decide how to create their vision board is critical to making this activity meaningful.

A vision board can be incredibly personal, so asking your students to share it with the class may limit the depth and honesty of the items on their boards. Instead of requiring students to share their vision boards publicly, you can invite them to record a short video describing one item on their vision board and what it represents to them.

Self-Management Strategy 2: Why, How, and What Goal-Setting Exercise

Setting goals is a powerful way to create clarity about what students care about and want to work to achieve. The focus of this why, how, and what goal-setting exercise is to identify one short-term self-management goal that students want to work toward. You may want to do this at the start of each week to encourage students to frame and focus their energy and effort in a particular direction. Simon Sinek's (2009) book *Start With Why* inspires the visual goal-setting map pictured in figure 6.4.

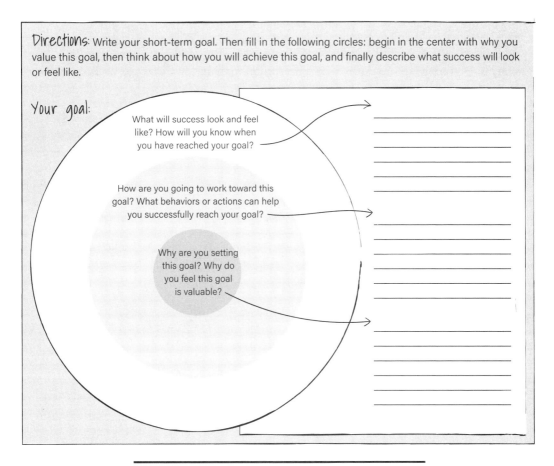

FIGURE 6.4: Why, how, and what short-term goal-setting exercise.

Students begin by articulating a single self-management goal. Then they start at the inner circle, and state the purpose or value of this particular goal. Why do they want to achieve this goal? Why is this goal valuable to them? Once students have written their why statements, they move to the middle circle to brainstorm specific actions and behaviors they believe will help them make progress toward this goal. Finally, they move to the outer circle to describe what they expect to feel or experience when they achieve this goal. Do they expect to feel something internally, or will there be an external reward of some kind?

Self-Management Strategy 3: Brain Breaks and Mood-Management Choice Board

As students get better at identifying their emotions, they must also learn how to manage them in productive and healthy ways. There are days when our students will be tired, emotional, or mentally distracted by what's happening in their lives beyond school; ignoring these feelings can be harmful (Kress & Elias, 2020).

One way to create space for these moments is to designate a physical location in your classroom as a brain-break or mood-management space. Online, a teacher can encourage students to take a five- or ten-minute brain and body break, walking away from the computer to stretch, snuggle with a pet, or listen to a favorite song. Students who need a break from academic or social engagement can use the space to engage in an activity to help them manage their feelings or stress. You can offer some options in the form of a choice board, as shown in the example in figure 6.5, for students to select from when they elect to go to this area of the classroom.

Responsible Decision-Making Skills

CASEL (n.d.) defines *responsible decision making* as the ability "to make caring and constructive choices about personal behavior and social interactions across diverse situations." Students make myriad decisions in a school day. They need to practice analyzing situations, weighing the pros and cons of particular responses or actions, and reflecting on their choices and how those choices impact the people around them. You can help students develop their responsible decision-making skills by asking them to reflect on their choices ("If I could do it differently"), engaging them in regular self-assessment activities, and providing them with opportunities to validate and celebrate the responsible choices their peers make.

Responsible Decision-Making Strategy 1: "If I Could Do It Differently" Reflection

When students make poor choices, you can institute a reflective practice called "If I could do it differently" to have them think about the choice they made and the impact of that choice on other people. Instead of simply taking a privilege away or isolating students, ask them to think about their actions and behaviors and why they were not conducive to maintaining a safe or productive learning environment. This reflection is designed to help students understand the impact of their choices and consider a different approach in the future.

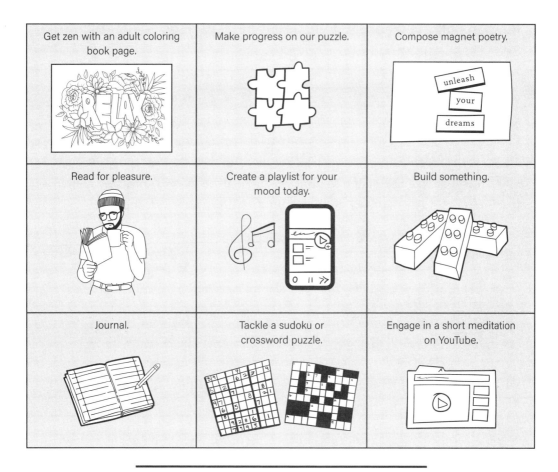

FIGURE 6.5: Mood-management choice board.

You can ask students to reflect on the following questions in a video recording, written reflection, or discussion with you.

- In their own words, what happened? What was the situation? What choice did they make?

- Why did they make this choice? What motivated them to act or behave in this way?

- How do they think their decision impacted other people in the learning community? How might it have made other people feel?

- If they could go back and make a different decision, what would they do and why?

- Is there something they can do now to lessen the negative impacts of their actions?

This type of reflection turns a misstep into an opportunity to learn, grow, and avoid similar mistakes in the future.

Responsible Decision-Making Strategy 2: Engage Students in Self-Assessment

As members of a blended learning community, students must actively engage in conversations and collaborate around shared tasks. This engagement is socially demanding and requires students to make many decisions when negotiating tasks with others. Employing a regular self-assessment practice following learning tasks that require interactions with others can increase students' awareness of their choices. The following is a list of questions you may want to consider asking students after their participation in a discussion to help them think critically about their decisions and actions.

- How engaged were they in today's discussion?
- How often did they participate?
- How prepared did they feel for today's discussion?
- What is one thing they felt they did well in today's discussion?
- What is one thing they would like to focus on improving during the next discussion?
- Describe one thing they did in the discussion that they think may have helped their classmates feel more comfortable sharing their ideas.

And after their engagement in a collaborative task, a selection of the following questions can help you encourage students to think critically about their decisions and actions.

- Describe their role in the group. What tasks or aspects of the assignment did they focus on? Why did they choose to focus on these aspects of the task?
- What strengths did they bring to the group task? What qualities or characteristics helped them contribute to the task in a meaningful way?
- What do they feel they need to work on when it comes to collaborative tasks? What qualities or characteristics make it challenging for them to engage in a group dynamic?
- What is one thing they felt they did well while working as part of a group?
- What is one thing they want to focus on improving the next time they work in a group?

Reflecting on their participation in a discussion or their contributions to a collaborative task reinforces the expectation that active engagement is their responsibility. It also encourages them to consider how the decisions they made during the conversation impacted other students. You can create a self-assessment document, digital form, or emoji scale and ask students to assess their participation in a small-group discussion or collaborative task, in person or online.

Responsible Decision-Making Strategy 3: Celebrating Each Other

Routines designed to help students celebrate and validate one another can strengthen a community and create visibility around the decisions and behaviors that positively impact others. You can dedicate time each Friday or the last Friday of each month to the practice of recognizing specific members of the community. This practice can take many forms. Following are some ideas for how you might facilitate this routine in your classroom or online.

- **Celebration circle:** Have students form a large circle in the classroom, and ask them to recognize the actions of another person in the circle that made them feel good or had a positive impact on them.

- **Kindness carousel:** Give all students a piece of paper, or assign them a digital slide in a class slide deck online. Ask them to write or type their name at the top of the paper or slide. Then give students time to add specific statements to each other's papers or digital documents. Encourage them to consider the following questions to ensure their messages to one another are meaningful.
  - ¤ What do they appreciate about this person? What do they do that has had a positive impact on them or the class community?
  - ¤ What qualities does this student possess that they admire or want to celebrate?
  - ¤ How has this person made them feel in their interactions?

- **Sentence starters:** In the early stages of providing positive peer feedback, providing sentence starters like the following examples may make this easier for students to do.
  - ¤ "Sarah was patient while working on . . ."
  - ¤ "I appreciated that Manuel . . ."
  - ¤ "I want to celebrate Chris because . . ."
  - ¤ "Jacqueline, I felt listened to when you . . ."

Reinforcing kind behaviors and responsible decision making with a celebration routine may motivate students to be more thoughtful in their interactions. The specific statements that students make about one another highlight the desirable behaviors and qualities and contribute to the development of the learning community.

Wrap-Up and Next Steps

The five SEL competencies that the CASEL framework identifies are a useful guide as you support students in developing the skills necessary to thrive in a dynamic, student-centered learning community. These skills can also help develop students' social presence in a blended learning environment so they can be comfortable projecting their social and emotional selves. A focus on cultivating relationship skills, self-awareness, social awareness, self-management, and responsible decision-making skills will support the development of affective expression, the expression of beliefs, feelings, and values; encourage open and honest communication; and foster a strong sense of group cohesion.

The COI framework emphasizes the importance of the social presence, or the students' ability to project their social identities in an online or blended learning environment. Building routines into your weekly work with students that focus on specific dimensions of SEL will strengthen your learning community, ensuring that students' work together is positive, productive, and meaningful. It will also provide students with invaluable life skills that will serve them long after they leave your class.

Developing a high-functioning learning community requires that you proactively teach students the skills they will need to flourish in that community. Since blended learning shifts control from teacher to learner and demands that students play an active role in the learning process, teaching these skills will support students in engaging with each other in a kind and supportive way.

Consider these next steps to help further your learning in this chapter. See also the reflection questions on page 144.

- Select one of the SEL competencies described in this chapter, and create a routine for your students to target the development of that competency. Consider the following questions as you design your routine.
    - ¤ What is the objective of this routine? What do you hope students will know or be able to do as a result of engaging in this activity?
    - ¤ What will you have students do? Describe the routine.
    - ¤ When will you engage students in this routine? Will it be daily, weekly, or monthly?

⌑ What scaffolds or supports will students need to engage in this routine successfully?

⌑ How will you collect feedback about the impact of this routine?

• You can use figure 6.6 to plan your routine.

Routine to help students develop the SEL competency of _____	
Objective:	
Description of routine:	
When students will engage in routine:	
Potential scaffolds or supports to provide:	
How feedback will be collected:	
Feedback received:	
Potential adjustments to make:	

FIGURE 6.6: SEL activity template.

*Visit **go.SolutionTree.com/technology** for a free reproducible version of this figure.*

Chapter 6: A Dynamic Learning Community— Reflect and Discuss

I encourage you to pause here to reflect on or discuss the following questions. If you are reading this book on your own, you can reflect on these questions in a blog post, publish your thoughts on your favorite social media platform, or capture your thoughts in a journal or notebook. If you are reading this book as part of a book club or book study, use the following questions to facilitate vibrant in-person or online discussions.

1. What words would you use to describe a thriving learning community? What qualities and characteristics help contribute to a positive and productive learning experience?

2. What has been your experience with SEL? How have you prioritized the cultivation of these skills in the past? How did the CASEL framework impact the way you think about SEL?

3. Which competency in the CASEL framework do you spend the most time and energy on in your work with students? How have you supported your students in developing this particular competency? What routines, activities, or tasks have been beneficial in targeting the development of this competency?

4. Which competency in the CASEL framework do you spend the least time and energy on in your work with students? Which strategy or strategies presented in this chapter can help you develop this particular competency? What routines, activities, or tasks do you think will be helpful in targeting the development of this competency?

5. How can a focus on SEL help you develop students' social presence in your blended learning environment? What impact would the development of these SEL competencies have on students' ability to authentically express themselves, engage in honest dialogue, and feel connected to other members of the community?

CHAPTER 7

THE 5E INSTRUCTIONAL MODEL AND STUDENT-CENTERED INQUIRY

While reading Matthew Lipman's (2003) book *Thinking in Education*, I was struck by his statement that young students begin their education in kindergarten "lively, curious, imaginative, and inquisitive" and "for a while they retain these wonderful traits. But then gradually a decline sets in and they become passive" (p. 12). His comment hit a nerve because I witnessed that shift in my son as he moved through school. I remember attending the Watch Me Work nights his Montessori preschool hosted twice a year. The students would show their parents around the classroom and engage with specific works or activities they enjoyed.

I remember my son gently pulled a placemat, stack of cards, and a magnifying glass off a shelf and carried it to our table. I watched as he used the magnifying glass to look for baby animals hidden in the images on the placemat. Each time he discovered one, he squealed with excitement and selected the corresponding card, which had a picture of the animal's parent. He'd place the card near the baby animal and rattle off the name of the animal and any information he knew about it: "Mama, that's a baby zebra. Did you know every zebra's stripes are different?" He was so engaged in the act of discovery; it was a joy to watch.

The joy evident in those early stages of learning dissipated with time. My son, who at the time of writing is in the seventh grade, does not enjoy school. He finds it tedious. The only redeeming quality of school from his perspective is the social dimension. He enjoys seeing his friends, though he has few opportunities to interact with them in the classroom. Like many students, he has been conditioned to comply with rigid rules; he receives few opportunities to direct his learning. He does not get to collaborate with his peers around high-interest topics or tasks. Instead, he spends his days listening to teacher-talk, following directions, and completing work in which he has little interest.

If you think about how teachers have classically delivered instruction, it should not surprise anyone that students lose their curiosity through the process of formal education (Berliner, 2020). They get answers to questions they did not ask and solutions to problems they have not encountered in life or had the opportunity to wrestle with themselves. As long as learning transmits in neat packages, it is unlikely to captivate students and nurture their innate curiosity and inquisitiveness. Learners need to engage in the messy work of constructing knowledge by asking questions, exploring complex topics, tinkering and testing, and generating solutions.

Student engagement and teacher engagement are reciprocal (Roth et al., 2007; Tucker, 2020b). As student engagement dips, it negatively impacts the teacher's level of engagement. So, it is in everyone's interest to keep engagement high with relevant and interesting learning experiences. Student-centered inquiry is a powerful vehicle to allow students to explore questions and topics of interest. That is why the cognitive presence is grounded in an inquiry cycle designed to move the learning community through the process of pursuing questions or problems at the core of the curriculum.

This chapter explores the cognitive presence, the final dimension of the COI framework, and how teachers can use the 5E instructional model (Bybee, 2014; Bybee et al., 2006) to blend active engagement online and offline to drive student-centered inquiry.

The Cognitive Presence

The cognitive presence is the dimension of the COI framework that focuses on students' ability to construct knowledge and make meaning as part of a learning community (Swan, 2019). Constructing knowledge requires the learner's active engagement and is the product of both individual and social processes. Individuals begin to make meaning through the process of exploration and reflection. They confirm and expand on their understanding through social engagement in discussion and collaboration around shared tasks (Garrison et al., 2001; Swan, 2019).

The cognitive presence is grounded in an inquiry cycle. The parts of the inquiry cycle, as pictured in figure 7.1, include a triggering event, exploration, integration, and resolution.

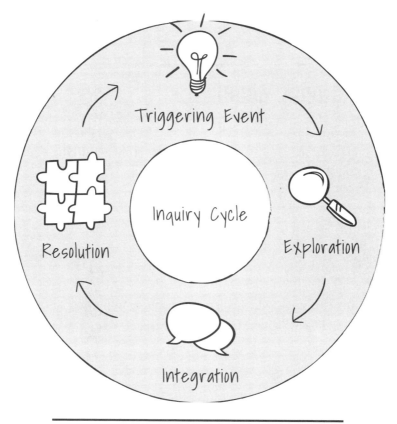

FIGURE 7.1: COI inquiry cycle.

The *triggering event* is the moment when learners encounter a problem, topic, or question that piques their interest and serves as the catalyst for the inquiry cycle. Once they have established a focus for the inquiry cycle, students move into *exploration*, where they attempt to learn about the problem, topic, or question. The exploration phase may be a more individual endeavor as students explore resources, research online, make observations, conduct interviews, and collect data via fieldwork. From exploration, students move into integration. *Integration* is the phase in the inquiry cycle when students test their new learning against the group. They engage in academic discourse to discuss their findings, and work collaboratively to make meaning. Integration requires that students make clear assertions, support their statements, ask questions, and listen actively. The final stage of the inquiry cycle is *resolution*, the point in the inquiry cycle where students take what they have learned and do something with it. They may reach conclusions, transfer their learning to a new situation, create a product to demonstrate their learning, or use what they have learned to design a solution. You can use an inquiry cycle to tap into your students' innate, though possibly dormant, curiosity and shift your students to the center of the learning process.

5E Instructional Model

The 5E instructional model can help you operationalize the inquiry process and aligns beautifully with the inquiry cycle at the heart of the COI. The 5E instructional model consists of these components.

1. **Engage:** This stage aligns with the triggering event, where student interest is piqued by a high-interest question or topic.

2. **Explore:** This stage is quite literally exploration, where students strive to develop an understanding of the question or topic.

3. **Explain:** This stage, which aligns to the integration phase of the inquiry cycle, challenges students to articulate what they learned, and listen actively to learn from one another.

4. **Elaborate:** This stage aligns to resolution, as students take what they learned and do something with it. They apply their learning to answer a question, solve a problem, or demonstrate their understanding.

5. **Evaluate:** This stage is the moment in the inquiry cycle where teachers measure student progress toward stated learning objectives. It is also a time for students to reflect on the process, and share feedback about their experience. It does not align with a specific stage of the cognitive presence but provides teachers and learners with an opportunity to better understand what was learned during the inquiry cycle.

The Biological Science Curriculum Study (BSCS) team and science educator Rodger W. Bybee (2014) developed the research-based 5E instructional model. Just as my definition of blended learning positions the learner as an active agent in the learning process, the 5E instructional model is grounded in constructivism and challenges students to take an active role in constructing their knowledge as they move through each E.

Although the 5E instructional model was initially developed for use in science education, it works across grade levels and content areas to create a clear structure that teachers can employ to design and facilitate student-centered inquiry. You can use an inquiry cycle grounded in the five Es to sequence a collection of lessons and be the sole focus of your students' work for two to three weeks. Presenting a topic or phenomenon as the focus of an inquiry cycle may grab some students' attention, but alternatively, you can design a 5E experience around an essential question, and have it run parallel to a traditional unit, providing your students with a deep dive into a high-interest question, issue, or topic related to the unit (Bybee, 2014).

Curriculum design experts Jay McTighe and Grant Wiggins' (2013) work on essential questions led me to use them as a starting place for a 5E inquiry cycle. McTighe and Wiggins (2013) emphasize the powerful role that essential questions can play in helping teachers organize their curriculum in a coherent way that is both engaging *and* deepens students' understanding of the content. They also highlight the role essential questions play in creating a class culture grounded in inquiry.

In their book *Essential Questions: Opening Doors to Student Understanding*, McTighe and Wiggins (2013) describe essential questions as:

- Being open ended
- Being thought provoking
- Engaging higher-order thinking
- Focusing on transferable ideas
- Leading to additional questions
- Requiring support and justification
- Recurring over time

There isn't a single or simple answer when students are working with an essential question. Students don't have to worry about being wrong. Instead, they can fully engage in the experience of wrestling with ideas and constructing knowledge, which lends itself well to the 5E instructional model.

If you are on a hybrid schedule that rotates students from synchronous in-person learning in the classroom and asynchronous remote learning at home, the 5E instructional model can also create meaningful student-centered learning that extends beyond the classroom to engage students as they work asynchronously at home and complement the work they do in class.

Regardless of the learning landscape you are working in, the strategies in this section will help you to create a student-centered experience grounded in inquiry. Let's review the purpose of each E and explore strategies you can use to weave together online and offline learning to make your student-centered investigations as interesting and engaging as possible.

Engage

The purpose of the Engage stage is to hook your students' attention, capturing their interest and capitalizing on their curiosity (Bybee, 2014). This first stage of the 5E is critical for maximizing student engagement, which will ultimately lead to better learning outcomes (Reckmeyer, 2019). You can present them with a question, a problem, or media designed to pique their interest. You may also use this initial stage of the inquiry cycle to assess your students' prior knowledge of a topic. Learning is not like lining up to run a race. Students do not stand shoulder to shoulder at a starting line. All students begin from a different place because of their individual life experiences. It is helpful to know where each student is beginning in terms of their prior knowledge, so you can make adjustments or provide useful resources during the explore stage to fill any gaps (Kilbane & Milman, 2014).

As students work individually or collaboratively to problem solve, brainstorm answers to the question posed, or engage with the media, you listen, observe, and note any misconceptions or gaps in knowledge. The more informal formative assessment data you collect during the first stage of this inquiry cycle, the more effective you will be at providing students the necessary support and guidance as they progress through the five Es.

You can adapt or use the following strategies—pique student interest with media and the "See/Think/Wonder" thinking routine, use a carousel brainstorm, and share prior knowledge in a discussion—to structure the Engage stage of your inquiry cycle.

Engage Strategy 1: Pique Interest With Media and the "See/Think/Wonder" Thinking Routine

You can begin by presenting students with a form of visual media: photographs, charts, graphics, video clips, infographics, political cartoons, artwork, and so on. Then ask them to explore this piece of visual media, make observations, and complete a "See/Think/Wonder" thinking routine, like the one pictured in figure 7.2. The "See/Think/Wonder" thinking routine is one of a collection developed by Project Zero (2019c) out of Harvard's Graduate School of Education that encourages students to develop their ability to think about their thinking by describing what they

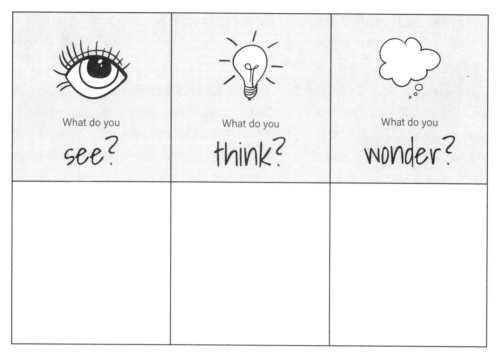

Source: Adapted from Project Zero, 2019c.

FIGURE 7.2: Project Zero thinking routine—"See/Think/Wonder."

*Visit **go.SolutionTree.com/technology** for a free reproducible version of this figure.*

see, what they are thinking about what they see, and what they are wondering about as they look at this visual.

You can ask your students to complete this thinking routine offline on paper or online in a digital document. You may also want to engage the entire class on a single digital slide deck where all students can capture their thinking on individual slides, and members of the class can see each other's responses.

Engage Strategy 2: Use a Carousel Brainstorm

Use a carousel brainstorm to engage students in activities like problem solving, sharing their thinking about particular vocabulary words, asking questions, and making predictions. For example, at the start of a 5E inquiry focused on a mathematical concept, you might mix unfamiliar mathematics problems with new mathematics vocabulary. Challenge students to add their thoughts to each poster, attempting to solve the unfamiliar problems and including words or drawings with the mathematics terms.

If you are working with students in a physical classroom, you can place poster paper in each of the four corners of the room with a problem, prompt, or vocabulary word on each. Then give students time to move around the room, adding their ideas to each poster. You may ask students to do this activity silently or encourage them to have conversations at each corner of the classroom.

If you engage your students online, you can create a digital carousel using a technology tool like Jamboard (https://jamboard.google.com) or a digital slide deck with a prompt on each slide. Just as the in-person carousel can happen silently or collaboratively, students online can work asynchronously on this task or work collaboratively in breakout rooms.

Engage Strategy 3: Share Prior Knowledge in a Discussion

You can tap into your students' prior knowledge via discussion. Put students in pairs or small groups for conversations in the classroom, or assign them to breakout rooms for this chat. If you want to engage your students asynchronously, you can ask them to respond to a prompt in a video- or text-based discussion. Regardless of the learning landscape you are using to engage students in sharing their prior knowledge, you want them to focus on answering the following questions.

- What do they already know about this concept, phenomenon, issue, process, or question?

- Where did they learn this information? Did they, for example, read a book, go on a trip, or chat with a friend or grandparent?

- What are they wondering about this topic, concept, phenomenon, issue, process, or question? What questions do you have about this topic, concept, phenomenon, issue, process, or question?

Explore

The purpose of the Explore stage is to encourage students to learn about the topic, concept, phenomenon, issue, process, or question. Exploration can take the form of offline experiential learning in students' environment or online reseach, both of which can help them develop a stronger understanding of topics, issues, and phenomenon. These position the learner as an active agent making meaning from direct experiences with people, places, and things both in person and online (Matriano, 2020). The exploration phase takes time and should not be rushed. Students need the space to explore and process new information and investigate a complex topic. If you push too hard at this stage, your students' understanding will be shallow. This creates a weak foundation for the rest of their progress through the five Es.

You can encourage students to learn about the topic or question at the heart of the 5E instructional model by engaging them in a number of exploratory activities, including the following.

- Conduct online research.

- Explore a teacher-curated collection of online resources.

- Make observations and document those observations with written descriptions, data tables, or drawings.

- Interview a classmate, friend, or family member.

- Conduct fieldwork to collect data.

- Experiment, tinker, or construct models to test ideas.

You can provide students with a multimodal experience during the Explore stage by combining online and offline exploration. You can ask students to conduct online research and interview someone in their lives to learn about a topic, or give them a collection of curated online resources and ask them to make observations. This combination of online and offline exploration reinforces the reality that students do not need to be connected to a device to learn. They can drive their learning offline.

You will also want to listen and observe students when they are exploring in class. If they are tinkering, experimenting, constructing a model, or researching a topic, you can gather informal data by circulating around the room and checking in with students. These informal data will help you provide scaffolds and support to aid students in effectively organizing the information they are gathering and analyzing. Graphic organizers, concept maps, sentence frames, and word banks with key vocabulary may be helpful in this phase.

You can adapt or use the following strategies—research teacher-curated online resources, make observations and document findings, and interview a family member or friend—to structure the Explore stage of your inquiry cycle.

Explore Strategy 1: Research Teacher-Curated Online Resources

Online research is an important life skill, but as with any skill, you must explicitly teach it. Students benefit from explicit instruction on how to conduct a savvy search, assess website credibility, and synthesize information from multiple sources (Nottage & Morse, 2021). Suppose you ask students to conduct online research to learn about a topic. In that case, you will want to spend time teaching them *how* to conduct a savvy search by using search operations, evaluating the credibility of websites, and properly citing sources. If your students are too young to conduct online research effectively, you can provide a collection of curated resources (for example, a collection of digital texts, websites, videos, or podcasts). Curated resources guarantee that students have access to high-quality, relevant information at a reading level that will be accessible for them.

As students conduct online research, you can support that process by providing a concept map or graphic organizer to capture their learning during their exploration. You may also use Project Zero's (2019a) "Connect, Extend, Challenge" thinking routine, as pictured in figure 7.3, to have students connect what they are learning to their prior knowledge, describe how the information they are encountering is extending their thinking on the topic, and identify aspects of this topic that are challenging, confusing, or causing them to wonder.

Connect	Extend	Challenge
How does this **connect** to what you already know?	What new ideas have **extended** your thinking on this topic?	What is **challenging** or confusing? What do you wonder?

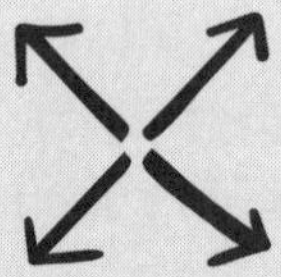

Source: Adapted from Project Zero, 2019a.

FIGURE 7.3: Project Zero thinking routine— "Connect, Extend, Challenge."

*Visit **go.SolutionTree.com/technology** for a free reproducible version of this figure.*

Explore Strategy 2: Make Observations and Document Findings

As students explore a question or investigate a phenomenon, you can encourage them to observe and document what they are noticing to learn about a topic. Students can observe behaviors or patterns at school, in their home environment, or outdoors. They can document their findings with detailed descriptions, data tables, sketches, or drawings.

Once students have captured their data via these observations, you can strategically pair or group them to share their findings with each other. What are the common patterns? Are there discrepencies or major differences in their data sets? What questions do they have after sharing their data?

After they finish discussing their individual findings, you can aske them to write a short reflection on what they learned. They may realize they need to spend more time collecting data or they may want to supplement their offline observations with online research.

Explore Strategy 3: Interview a Family Member or Friend

Students can collect qualitative data and learn a great deal from engaging in conversation with the people around them. Friends, parents, grandparents, and classmates can provide insight into various topics, phenomena, and questions. Ask your students to work in pairs or small groups to craft questions related to their investigation topic. You may also want to provide links to interview questions online for them to modify and use. Then have them identify one or two people in their lives who they can interview to learn more about the topic. They can use digital tools, like voice recording (with permission from the subjects), to capture the content of their conversations for future reference and accurate citations. These interviews may take place in the classroom if students are interviewing one another or members of another class. Alternatively, they can take place online outside of school via Zoom or FaceTime if students are interviewing family members or friends.

You can ask students to complete a 3-2-1 activity (see figure 7.4, page 158) to share what they learned during their interviews. Ask them to share three interesting or important facts or details, two connections they were able to make or two questions they have, and one surprising thing. You can modify the prompts attached to each number based on what you think would be most beneficial for you and your students. Students can fulfill this exercise on paper, a digital document, or a shared slide deck.

Three details, facts, or things you learned	1.
	2.
	3.
Two questions you have	1.
	2.
One thing that surprised you	1.

FIGURE 7.4: 3-2-1 post-interview reflection.

*Visit **go.SolutionTree.com/technology** for a free reproducible version of this figure.*

As students explore and investigate, your focus should be on supporting the process by explicitly teaching them skills to ensure this phase of the 5E instructional model is as productive and positive as possible. Your instruction may include helping students develop and refine their research, interview, or fieldwork skills.

Explain

The purpose of the Explain stage is to challenge students to articulate their learning and share their discoveries. This stage requires that students present their ideas in a clear and cogent way, put complex ideas and vocabulary in their own words, make connections between key concepts, and support their statements with details and facts they learn during their exploration. When students are able to generate a clear explanation, they learn more and are more likely to be able to transfer their learning to new and novel situatons (Sparks, 2013). In turn, they must also practice their listening skills as they hear what other members of the class discover during their explorations. The Explain phase is an opportunity for students to learn with and from each other, so you want to create space for students to engage with one another either synchronously in small groups or asynchronously in a video- or text-based online discussion.

At this stage of the inquiry cycle, you can also spend time introducing important information, unpacking complex concepts, and providing clarification either in differentiated direct instruction in small groups as part of a station rotation, a mini-lesson for the whole class as part of a whole-group rotation, or asynchronously via video instruction. This is an opportunity for you to support the learning with instruction and modeling to ensure students understand the most important information.

You can adapt or use the following strategies—record video explanations, discuss in small groups, and write or visually depict explanations—to structure the Explain stage of your inquiry cycle.

Explain Strategy 1: Record Video Explanations

There are several advantages to having students record video explanations using a platform like FlipGrid instead of presenting live. First, they have more control over the experience. They can re-record if their initial recording isn't as smooth or clear as they would like. It may remove some of the anxiety and social pressure students feel when speaking live in front of their peers, yielding more substantial explanations.

In turn, when students are watching each other's videos, they can self-pace through their peers' explanations by pausing, rewinding, and rewatching. This may make it easier to learn from one another. If the platform allows, you should encourage them to post comments, ask questions, and make connections between details shared in their classmates' videos and their own discoveries. You should provide explicit instruction about the strategies students can use to reply thoughtfully and substantively to each other. For example, students can build on an idea shared, make connections, respectfully disagree or offer a different perspective, or share a personal story (Tucker, 2012). Their responses should reflect higher-order thinking to ensure they are learning with and from each other. Students might respond with statement like the following.

- "Marco's comment about the impact of social media on attention spans made me think about . . ."
- "Alejandra's point that oil isn't sustainable long term is valid, but I believe . . ."
- "I had a similar experience to Maddox when I was observing . . ."

Explain Strategy 2: Discuss in Small Groups

Instead of facilitating a whole-group share-out, which is time consuming and likely to bore students, you can break the class into four groups. Then you can have each group meet in one of the four corners of the classroom (or in virtual breakout rooms), arrange their chairs in a circle, and take turns sharing what they learned or discovered (see chapter 5, page 111, for more about four-corner conversations). This smaller group dynamic gives all in the group the time and space to share what they learned without the pressure of the entire class staring at them. You can also encourage students to pause after each person shares and spend a couple of minutes discussing each new contribution.

Explain Strategy 3: Write or Visually Depict Explanations

If an in-class or online discussion is not possible, you can ask students to express their learning in a piece of writing or visually with a flowchart, concept map, infographic, or sketchnotes. Since different students will gravitate to different forms of expression, you can provide them with meaningful choices by allowing them to select from a collection of options. Research has shown that learner variability is the norm, not the exception, so giving students meaningful choice about how they communicate their learning makes them feel more confident in communicating their learning (Meier & Rossi, 2020; Novak & Tucker, 2021).

Your focus during the Explain phase is to listen to your students to identify gaps and misconceptions that surface as they share what they learned. Depending on the age of the students, you may also want to play a role in facilitating the sharing of ideas to ensure the conversations are equitable and all students have the opportunity to be heard. The Stanford Teaching Commons (n.d.) makes the point that "equitable class participation doesn't just happen, it takes deliberate and attentive practices. Oftentimes some individuals might dominate group discussions, while other perspectives remain underrepresented." One strategy teachers can use to create more equitable conversations with students of all ages is to assign students a role within the group, like a first speaker, facilitator, questioner, scribe, and equity monitor (Stanford Teaching Commons, n.d.). This encourages students to take an active role in driving, monitoring, and engaging in the discussion.

In addition, students may need support in the form of sentence starters or prompts to help them feel confident in presenting their ideas. You can also run a short demonstration by asking a few students to role-play using a collection of prompts.

As students engage in real-time discussions, you can circulate around the room (or briefly visit virtual breakout rooms), listening to the ideas and information they are sharing. But with video responses and asynchronous replies, you will want to spend time watching their videos to understand what they think they learned during their exploration. Just as video responses make it easier for students to self-pace through others' videos and leave comments, you will have more time to listen and learn if you have a collection of your students' video responses.

Elaborate

The purpose of the Elaborate stage is to extend and enrich students' understanding of the concepts or skills at the heart of the 5E inquiry cycle by challenging them to transfer or "apply learning to a new situation beyond the context in which it was learned" (McTighe, Doubet, & Carbaugh, 2020, p. 5). Transferring new learning to a novel situation provides invaluable insight into students' level of understanding. This stage of the 5E instructional model is cognitively challenging and, like the Explore stage, should not be rushed. Students will also benefit from peer support as they attempt to apply their learning. Designing elaborate activities to prioritize collaboration among students is likely to make the students' work of transferring their learning more successful.

In addition to transferring their learning, you can ask students to make connections or engage in review and practice. It is evident that the process of making connections between prior and new knowledge, identifying the links between concepts learned, and orienting new learning in a larger context helps students retain what they learned (Sekeres et al., 2016). The review and practice can help reinforce students' understanding of key vocabulary, concepts, and skills.

Your focus during the Elaborate stage is to serve as a facilitator or coach supporting students as they make connections, practice, and apply. You may need to offer individuals or small groups feedback and support as they attempt to take what they learned and transfer that learning to a new situation. This support may involve check-in conversations, reteaching, and designing additional scaffolds or resources to support students.

You can use or adapt the following strategies—make connections with a concept map, implement the "Tell Me How" challenge, and use a performance task choice board—to structure the Elaborate stage of your inquiry cycle.

Elaborate Strategy 1: Make Connections With a Concept Map

You can ask students to reflect on their learning and make connections in a visible format like a concept map. The goal of the concept map is to relate concepts in a cognitive structure by organizing new information and creating connections between ideas and prior knowledge, related concepts, and links to the world beyond the classroom (Ausubel, 2012; Roessger, Daley, & Hafez, 2018). Depending on the level of support your students need, you can provide a preformatted concept map (on paper or digitally) or encourage them to create their own structure or combine text and drawings to capture their thinking. See figure 7.5 for an example.

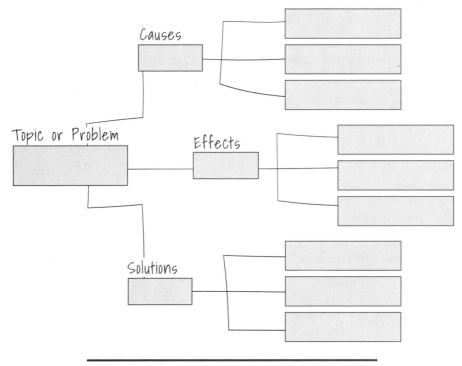

FIGURE 7.5: Concept map.

*Visit **go.SolutionTree.com/technology** for a free reproducible version of this figure.*

Concept maps highlight the students' big takeaways from the learning but may also reveal misconceptions and gaps in knowledge. You can encourage students to learn from each other and provide peer feedback if they post images of their concept maps on a digital sticky note board or insert those images into a shared class slide deck.

Elaborate Strategy 2: Implement the "Tell Me How" Challenge

Present your students with a novel or real-world scenario, problem, or task and ask them to apply what they have learned to that situation. Once they have had an opportunity to think about how they would attempt to solve that problem or complete that task, ask them to record a video walking you through their process. The goal of this activity is to surface their thinking, not necessarily produce an answer.

For example, you might present students with a quirky, high-interest, real-world mathematics problem and ask them to explain how they would solve that problem. YummyMath.com has a collection of questions designed to spark creative problem solving in mathematics. In advance of the Super Bowl, YummyMath features a problem challenging students to find the mean, median, and mode of losing scores, winning scores, and range of scores from previous Super Bowl games and make predictions about what they think will happen in the current year's game. Once students work individually or collaboratively to complete a real-world mathematics challenge, they record a short explanation of their mathematical thinking and reasoning, using questions like the following to guide their thinking.

- What steps would they move through to solve this problem?
- What strategies would they use? Why would they use these specific strategies?
- What questions do they have now?

Similarly, a third-grade science teacher could challenge students to observe a scientific phenomenon they are learning about, such as the reflection of light, decomposition of organic matter, or cause-and-effect relationship of magnetic interactions. Then ask students to answer questions like the following.

- What are they noticing as they observe this phenomenon?
- What is changing and why?
- How is this phenomenon part of a system? Describe how the system works.

This exercise can provide invaluable insight into what your students know about a process while highlighting areas of confusion that you may need to address.

Elaborate Strategy 3: Use a Review and Practice Choice Board

You can design a choice board to build student agency into the Elaborate phase of this investigation. You may want students to make connections, review essential vocabulary or concepts, and transfer their learning via a performance task. However, not all students will enjoy making connections, reviewing information, or practicing skills the same way, so a choice board provides them with meaningful options. You can create a choice board with three columns and have each column focus on a particular type of learning activity, as shown in figure 7.6 (page 164).

Choose an item from each column to prepare for the assessment.

Make Connections	Review and Practice	Apply Your Learning
Compose a poem or song	Online discussion	Writing
Select at least five vocabulary words from this unit that you need to spend time working with, and write a poem or song that uses these words.	Post a response to the online discussion about a major concept in this unit. In your post, identify the concept you want to focus on, describe its key characteristics, and discuss its significance in this unit. Then reply to at least two other members of the class.	Write an argumentative paragraph taking a position on an important issue presented in this unit. Make a clear claim, support your claim with relevant evidence, and explain how your evidence supports your claim.
Online review	Create a concept map	Speaking and listening
Log in to Quizlet, and create a digital review for at least five of your vocabulary words and definitions in your own words. Once you've created your digital review, spend time practicing the words.	Identify three big concepts that we covered in this unit, and create a concept map to show what you know about these concepts. What are their key characteristics? How do they relate to one another?	Find a partner to engage in a discussion with about a topic that is central to this unit. Take turns discussing the following. 1. What did you know about this topic before the unit? 2. What did you learn about the topic during the unit? 3. What are you still wondering about?
Teach someone	Make a comparison	Active reading
Create a video teaching at least five of your vocabulary words to a younger learner who is unfamiliar with them. Make sure to include visuals and text in your video.	Think of an analogy you can make between a major concept in this unit and something else you think it shares key characteristics with, and either describe your analogy in writing or use side-by-side labeled drawings to make the comparison clear.	Find a digital text on a topic or issue that is central to this unit. Actively read by annotating, drawing sketchnotes, or completing a 3-2-1 reflection, listing three things you learned, two connections you were able to make, and one thing that surprised you.

FIGURE 7.6: Review and practice choice board.

*Visit **go.SolutionTree.com/technology** for a free reproducible version of this figure.*

Within each column, you can give students three options for how they might complete that activity. In the Make Connections column, you can let students decide if they want to make connections in writing, engage in a discussion, or complete a concept map to surface the big ideas and analyze the relationships between them. You can use the Review and Practice column to provide both online and offline options since some students may prefer a more tactile offline experience. In contrast, others may prefer to log into a computer program for practice. In the Apply your Learning column, you can present three performance tasks that ask students to transfer their learning to different scenarios. Alternatively, you can provide three different options for performing or sharing their learning (for example, written response, video recording, or constructing a model).

Evaluate

The purpose of the Evaluate stage is to measure student progress toward learning objectives. What do you want students to know, understand, or be able to do at the end of this inquiry cycle? How successful was this 5E instructional model at moving students toward those objectives? Given the student-centered nature of this inquiry cycle, how can you build agency into the assessment to allow students the opportunity to decide how they will best express and communicate their learning? You may want to explore using performance tasks or projects to measure your students' understanding of key concepts or mastery of specific skills. Compared to traditional tests, these authentic forms of assessment are more likely to yield products that provide insight into what your students know and can do (McTighe et al., 2020).

In addition to assessing their learning, you will want to encourage a reflective practice to help students intentionally think about their learning. Following are some questions you may want to ask students to reflect on.

- What did they learn? Can they identify a specific concept or skill?
- How did they learn it? Describe the process.
- Which E was beneficial in the process of understanding this concept or mastering this skill?
- What questions or wonderings do they still have?
- Did this inquiry cycle spark additional questions?

Dedicating time to reflection at the end of an inquiry cycle helps students appreciate the impact of this work on their skill set or level of understanding. It can also provide insight into the questions or wonderings that still exist that you may need to address.

In addition to assessment and reflection, you can wrap up a 5E instructional model by gathering feedback from students about their experience. When using a new model, the best way to identify what is working and what is not is by asking students to provide you with feedback. Consider asking them the following questions.

- What did they enjoy most about this experience? Was there an activity or task they found particularly interesting or engaging?

- What did they find most challenging about this experience? Was there an activity or task they struggled with or found frustrating?

- How interesting was the essential question or topic? Is there another question or topic they would have enjoyed investigating?

- Did they feel like they needed more support during any of the five Es? What type of support would have been helpful?

- How did the pace of their progress through the five Es feel? Did they have enough time with each task or too much time?

- Did they feel like they could demonstrate or show what they learned in a way that worked well for them? If not, how would they have enjoyed sharing their learning?

- What recommendations or suggestions would they make for another 5E inquiry cycle?

The students' responses can shed light on the aspects of this experience that you should retain in the future while providing suggestions for modifying and improving it moving forward.

Your focus during the Evaluate stage is to support the transfer process with teacher check-ins, scaffolds designed to support the process, and focused, actionable feedback. You also measure the effectiveness of this inquiry cycle in helping students make progress toward specific learning objectives. These learning objectives, informed by your grade-level and content-area standards, can serve as the foundation for the rubric you use to assess student progress. If you align the criteria on your rubric to specific standards, skills, or learning objectives, it does not matter which project or performance task students select. You can use the same rubric to assess all of your students' final products because you assess specific standards and skills, not the product itself. Some students might deliver a TED-style talk while others choose to make a documentary, but you evaluate the depth of understanding and quality of evidence or support in those products, not the specific aspects of public speaking or video production.

You can use or adapt the following strategies—provide a project choice board, offer a "Would you rather?" choice, and use a three-part exit ticket—to structure the Evaluate stage of your inquiry cycle.

Evaluate Strategy 1: Provide a Project Choice Board

You can provide students with a collection of project structures to choose from to express and communicate their learning. As pictured in figure 7.7, the project options should attempt to appeal to different types of learners. Some students might enjoy taking what they learned and crafting a short TED-style talk to answer

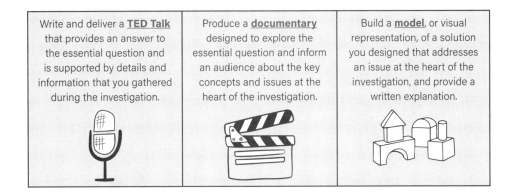

| Write and deliver a **TED Talk** that provides an answer to the essential question and is supported by details and information that you gathered during the investigation. | Produce a **documentary** designed to explore the essential question and inform an audience about the key concepts and issues at the heart of the investigation. | Build a **model**, or visual representation, of a solution you designed that addresses an issue at the heart of the investigation, and provide a written explanation. |

FIGURE 7.7: 5E project choice board example.

the essential question, pulling together everything they learned into a cogent and compelling live or recorded presentation. Other students might prefer to produce a documentary conveying to an audience insight into the essential question and what they learned about it through the inquiry cycle. Finally, some students who enjoy more tactile tasks can build a model or visual representation of a solution designed to address an issue or answer the question, then provide a clear written explanation for their design. Regardless of the project structure students select, they may benefit from supports and scaffolds to help them think through the parts of the project before they get started. In each option, you can link to a supporting document designed to support them in the early stages of planning their projects. These digital support documents, which are indicated by the underlined words, can help you ensure students are making progress, and identify students who might need additional support.

Depending on the age of your students, you can have them select from any number of activities that might include writing a children's story, designing an infographic or digital poster, creating a multimedia slideshow, or producing an original podcast. Students can produce a variety of products that will challenge them to analyze and synthesize what they learned during the 5E inquiry cycle and share it with an audience of their peers. Once students have completed a project of their choice, you can facilitate a gallery walk or exhibition to allow students the time to explore each other's work, learn from each other, and provide meaningful feedback.

Evaluate Strategy 2: Offer a "Would You Rather?" Choice

If you want students to complete a performance task, you can give them a "Would you rather?" choice between two situations that challenge them to apply their learning, as pictured in figure 7.8. Performance tasks provide an authentic context and ask students to assume a specific role as they approach the situation. Even a simple choice between two scenarios may help students feel more confident transferring their learning to create something that demonstrates their concept knowledge or skill set. For example, a world history teacher might present students with the two historical thinking scenarios such as those in figure 7.8 to assess how well they can analyze primary and secondary sources to reach conclusions about a particular era in history, like the Industrial Revolution. The two scenarios give students the choice to read and write or to analyze visual media and draw, which provides students with agency to decide which scenario will allow them to effectively communicate their thinking.

Historical Thinking Scenario 1	Historical Thinking Scenario 2
Read these primary and secondary source articles about the Industrial Revolution and write an informational essay using details from the sources to identify the factors that led to the Industrial Revolution, describe the impact on daily life, and analyze the effect on society more generally.	Analyze this collection of political cartoons from the Industrial Revolution, noting details from each that reveal important causes and effects of the Industrial Revolution. Then use what you have learned to create two political cartoons to be featured side-by-side that depict life before with life during the Industrial Revolution.

FIGURE 7.8: "Would you rather?" performance tasks.

*Visit **go.SolutionTree.com/technology** for a free reproducible version of this figure.*

Once students have completed their performance tasks, you can strategically pair students who selected the same performance task to present their approaches to each other and receive feedback. They can compare and discuss their work. How did they each approach the task? Were there similarities and differences in their approaches? What might they do differently if they approached a similar task in the future?

Evaluate Strategy 3: Use a Three-Part Exit Ticket

You can also wrap up a 5E instructional model with a three-part exit ticket that combines assessment, reflection, and feedback questions, like the open-ended digital form example pictured in figure 7.9. But you can also design more specific questions to assess students' understanding and challenge them to articulate their learning in clear written responses. For example, a teacher wrapping up an inquiry

---

Evaluate: Exit Ticket

What concept or skill did you learn during this 5E instructional cycle?

Your answer

How did you learn it? What activities or tasks were most useful in helping you to understand this concept or apply this skill?

Your answer

What questions or wonderings do you still have about the topic of this inquiry?

Your answer

Is there any aspect of this 5E inquiry cycle that you wish we could have spent more time on?

Your answer

What was most challenging about this inquiry cycle? What additional supports might have made this part of the cycle easier to complete or navigate?

Your answer

What suggestions or recommendations would you make if we were to use the 5E inquiry cycle to explore another essential question?

Your answer

FIGURE 7.9: Example of three-part exit ticket digital form.

cycle focused on photosynthesis or animal habitats might include questions about vocabulary, concepts, or processes more specific to those topics.

Written responses that are required to include details, reasoning, and justification are more likely to provide an accurate picture of what students know, understand, or can do compared to multiple-choice or true-false questions. You can follow the assessment questions with reflective prompts that ask students to think about their learning during this inquiry cycle. Finally, you can end the exit ticket with questions designed to help you learn about your students' experience and figure out what worked and what might need to be modified before using the 5E instructional model again.

Wrap-Up and Next Steps

Even though the 5E instructional model is not included in the official taxonomy of blended learning models, you can use this approach to student-centered inquiry to effectively blend active, engaged learning online with active, engaged learning offline. The goal of the 5E instructional model is to position students at the center of learning and ignite their curiosity.

Your role during this student-centered investigation is to act as a facilitator and coach: listening, observing, and supporting. Your students may also need explicit instruction on academic and interpersonal skills to successfully progress through a 5E inquiry cycle.

You can also focus on increasing student agency by incorporating at least one meaningful choice at each stage of the 5E inquiry with a "Would you rather?" choice that presents two options. Even a simple choice can have a powerful impact on student motivation and engagement.

As you design your 5E instructional model, strive to balance the online and offline learning and the individual and collaborative tasks. This balance will allow for both individual learning and social learning, which combine to create a rich experience as students investigate a question or topic.

Consider the following next steps to further your learning in this chapter. See also the reflection questions on page 173.

- Use the 5E instructional model to design a student-centered inquiry cycle you can use during your next unit. Select an essential question you generated in response to question 2 in the Reflect and Discuss section to drive your inquiry cycle. Identify the target standards and craft clear learning objectives to guide your work as you design this experience.

- Once you have a clear sense of the learning objectives students will work toward, use the template in figure 7.10 to design each of the

Target standard or standards:
Learning objectives:
Essential question or topic:

Engage	
Directions: Links and resources:	Your work:

Explore	
Directions: Links and resources:	Your work:

· Explain	
Directions: Links and resources:	Your work:

Elaborate	
Directions: Links and resources:	Your work:

Evaluate	
Directions: Links and resources:	Your work:

Rubric:

Criteria	1—Beginning	2—Developing	3—Proficient	4—Mastery

FIGURE 7.10: 5E instructional model template.

*Visit **go.SolutionTree.com/technology** for a free reproducible version of this figure.*

five Es using strategies described in this chapter. Feel free to modify or rework strategies so they are appropriate for your grade level, content area, and population of learners. Review the purpose of each E to ensure the strategies and the learning activities at each stage of the inquiry cycle will effectively meet those objectives.

- Decide on an assessment strategy that you believe will provide insight into your students' progress toward the stated learning objectives. Consider giving your students agency to make a decision about how they communicate and share their learning. Then use your target standards to develop a four-point rubric to assess students' level of mastery in relation to those standards.

- Once you have developed your 5E inquiry cycle, share it with a colleague or your collaborative team for feedback. What are their thoughts on your essential question? Would they recommend you add or edit anything at each stage of the inquiry cycle? Are there places where additional scaffolds or incorporating student agency would make this experience more accessible? Do they think the assessment strategy aligns with the learning objectives? Are there any suggestions they have for refining the rubric you will use to assess student work? Incorporate their feedback to refine your inquiry cycle before using it with your students.

Chapter 7: The 5E Instructional Model and Student-Centered Inquiry—Reflect and Discuss

I encourage you to pause here to reflect on or discuss the following questions. If you are reading this book on your own, you can reflect on these questions in a blog post, publish your thoughts on your favorite social media platform, or capture your thoughts in a journal or notebook. If you are reading this book as part of a book club or book study, use the following questions to facilitate vibrant in-person or online discussions.

1. What form has inquiry taken in your class? How often do students get to engage in inquiry and investigate a high-interest topic? What is both challenging and rewarding about facilitating student-centered inquiry?

2. Think about your next unit and brainstorm relevant, high-interest essential questions that might yield a strong 5E investigation. Could this 5E instructional model be the sole focus of your work with students for two to three weeks? Or would it run parallel to a traditional unit and provide a deep dive into a topic related to an existing unit?

3. Which of the Engage activities were you most drawn to and why? How might you modify this activity for your grade level, content area, or population of learners? What supports and scaffolds might they need to successfully engage in this activity?

4. What forms of exploration would work best for your grade level, content area, or population of learners? If you were going to select one online and one offline exploration activity to help students learn about a topic, which would you choose and why? What specific skills might you need to explicitly teach them to ensure they would be successful during this stage of the 5E?

5. How would you like students to explain what they learned or discovered? Would you facilitate synchronous small-group discussions or ask them to post synchronous responses online? What barriers might exist when you ask students to share in small groups or online? How might you strive to remove those barriers to ensure all students feel confident expressing their learning?

6. Which of the strategies described in the Elaborate stage was the most appealing? How might you modify this activity for your grade level, content area, or population of learners? What supports and scaffolds might they need to successfully engage in this activity?

7. What are the advantages and potential drawbacks of using projects and performance tasks to assess student progress toward learning objectives at the end of a 5E? Which type of assessment are you most drawn to and why? How might you build student agency into the assessment process?

CHAPTER 8

HOW TO TAKE BLENDED LEARNING TO THE NEXT LEVEL

My blended learning journey began with online discussions. As a student, I found class discussions engaging, thought provoking, and informative. Yet, as a teacher, I found it almost impossible to engage my students in the kind of vibrant discussions I believed were central to the meaning-making process. Online discussions offered a new avenue to encourage students to participate in academic discourse.

My first foray into online discussions was rocky. My questions were basic analytical prompts that likely didn't stir much excitement or curiosity. I quickly realized that students needed explicit instruction on participating in substantive and meaningful communication online. I developed specific strategies to support them in saying something substantial and provided a collection of sentence frames to guide their replies to each other. I set aside class time and encouraged students to self-critique the quality of their online posts and replies to peers, bringing a critical eye to their work.

As my students developed their proficiency in their conversations online, I began to expand how I used our asynchronous discussion. I realized there were myriad ways to use online discussions. Students would engage in lively debates about issues and current events. They would write and post short narratives using our vocabulary words and provide each other with specific feedback on narrative elements and word usage. When groups of students read their books for literature circles (a strategy for giving students meaningful choice about what they read that allows *them* to drive the book discussion; Ferdiansyah, Ridho, Sembilan, & Zahro, 2020), they developed their discussion questions and chatted about aspects of their book that interested them. They would crowdsource information about the historical context of a novel from online research and share it in our online discussions. Over time and with much experimentation, I realized how versatile an online discussion space could be.

Just as my use of online discussions expanded and evolved, so will your understanding and use of the various blended learning models. You'll find that the models are simply a starting point. The taxonomy of blended learning models gives you a collection of helpful structures to begin with. As you develop your confidence and proficiency, you'll discover variations that can increase student agency, provide more opportunities for differentiation, and allow students more control over the pace of their learning. You will find that even though blended learning does not equate to personalized learning, you can leverage the models to create more time to work one on one with students.

This chapter reviews some of the next-level considerations that will help you go farther in your blended learning practice. Once you have a firm understanding of the models and feel comfortable using them to design and facilitate learning, you'll have the bandwidth to increase the level of intentionality in your design work. You can begin to think about using formative assessment to drive differentiation, differentiating content, process, and products, balancing lesson elements, strategically pairing the learning activity with a synchronous or asynchronous mode, and thinking outside the box when it comes to the models.

Formative Assessment Drives Differentiation

Formative assessment provides a window into your students' progress as they move toward clear learning objectives and goals. Unlike summative assessment, which occurs at the end of a learning cycle, *formative assessment* is often informal and designed to take the temperature of the learning as it is happening (Heritage, 2013; Elmahdi, Al-Hattami, & Fawzi, 2018). There are three moments in a learning cycle when you want to collect formative assessment data: (1) assessing prior knowledge before instruction starts, (2) checking for understanding during instruction, and (3) engaging students in self-assessment and reflection after instruction is complete. Then the self-assessment routines that challenge students to think critically about their work and evaluate their progress toward stated learning objectives, combined with a reflective practice, can help students identify wha they need to spend more time and energy on in the next learning cycle. From a teacher perspective, this takes some of the guesswork out of planning the next unit because students are communicating what they need and would benefit from spending more time on in the next learning cycle. Teachers can build these moments into a complete learning cycle, as pictured in figure 8.1.

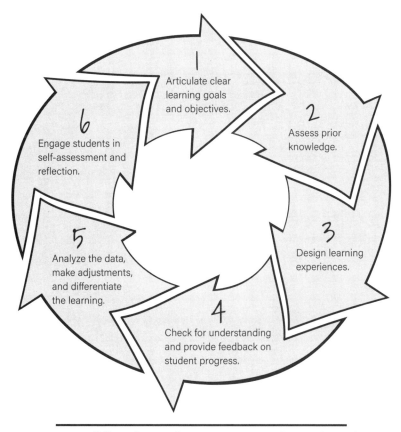

FIGURE 8.1: Building formative assessment into a learning cycle.

The more mechanisms you build into the learning to collect formative assessment data, the more successful you'll be answering the following questions.

- What do students know or understand?
- What are students able to do?
- What gaps, misconceptions, and errors are evident in students' work?
- What support do students need to continue making progress?
- Is additional instruction, reteaching, or modeling necessary?

The answers to these questions make it possible to more effectively differentiate instruction, provide targeted feedback, design appropriate supports and scaffolds, and adjust the level of academic rigor and complexity of what you are asking students to do.

Let's review the moments in a learning cycle—before, during, and after—when you can collect formative assessment data. I'll also provide specific strategies you can use at each point in the learning cycle to collect informal data to better understand where individual students are in their progress.

Before the Learning: Assess Prior Knowledge

Once you have articulated clear learning objectives and goals to clarify what students are working toward, you can assess prior knowledge before you begin your design work. These data will help you design learning experiences that meet students where they are in terms of their current knowledge, skills, and abilities. Assessing prior knowledge can also reveal misconceptions and gaps as well as areas of proficiency that you do not need to invest significant instructional time in developing.

The following strategies—give entrance tickets, use a sort-it-out activity, and hold four-minute talks—can help you assess prior knowledge in your students before instruction.

Assessing Prior Knowledge Strategy 1: Give Entrance Tickets

Design a simple entrance ticket, like that pictured in figure 8.2, to act as a preassessment that allows you to assess what students already know or think about a topic. Ask questions to encourage students to share their prior knowledge and its source, identify aspects of the topic they are interested in or curious about, and explain what they think key vocabulary words mean in their own words.

Assessing Prior Knowledge Strategy 2: Use a Sort-It-Out Activity

Provide students with a collection of images and words related to a topic, text, or unit they are about to study. Then ask them to sort it out—that is, make sense of them. Challenge them to create a concept map, flowchart, or sequence that makes sense to them. Give them time to work with the images and words to apply what they already know and impose order on the collection of images and words. Once they are done, ask them to either record a short video or produce a written response to articulate their thought process and explain why they organized the images and words in a particular order or using a specific format. This exercise can be done individually, in pairs, or collaboratively in small groups to reveal what students think they know about concepts at the heart of a unit they are about to begin.

Assessing Prior Knowledge Strategy 3: Hold Four-Minute Talks

Pair students in class or virtual breakout rooms for a quick chat to discuss what they know about a topic, concept, or skill. Explain that one student in each pair will

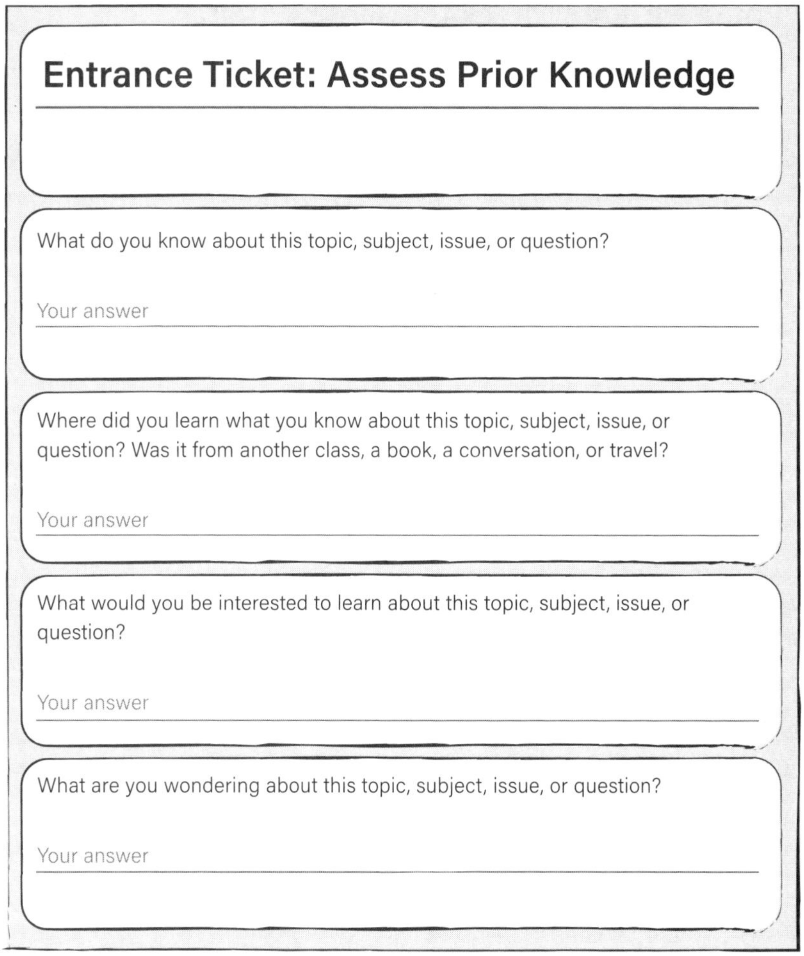

Entrance Ticket: Assess Prior Knowledge

What do you know about this topic, subject, issue, or question?

Your answer

Where did you learn what you know about this topic, subject, issue, or question? Was it from another class, a book, a conversation, or travel?

Your answer

What would you be interested to learn about this topic, subject, issue, or question?

Your answer

What are you wondering about this topic, subject, issue, or question?

Your answer

FIGURE 8.2: Example of digital entrance ticket to assess prior knowledge.

go first. These students have exactly two minutes to share what they think they know about this topic, skill, or concept and where they learned it. The person who is not speaking must focus on actively listening and making mental or written notes of important points. Once the first two minutes are up, provide students with a signal to switch roles. As students engage in these quick conversations, you can circulate around the room or pop into and out of breakout rooms to listen and observe. This provides some general information about the group's prior knowledge.

If you are working in an asynchronous mode with students, you can use an online discussion prompt instead of live four-minute talks to gather information about what students know about a topic.

During the Learning: Check for Understanding

As students engage with ideas, information, and strategies, you want to build mechanisms into that experience that will enable both you and your students to check for understanding. This can happen informally as you listen to and observe students at work. For example, building discussion, feedback, practice, and application into a teacher-led station can help you better understand students' progress toward comprehending key concepts and mastering specific skills. Technology can also help you quickly gather and save informal data as students work to better understand where they are at in their progress toward specific learning goals and objectives.

The following strategies—create an analogy, engage in error analysis, and rate your understanding—can help check for understanding during instruction.

Checking for Understanding Strategy 1: Create an Analogy

Ask your students to make a comparison or create an analogy between a new concept or skill they are learning and something else in their lives that is familiar. An analogy or comparison challenges students to think about the qualities or characteristics of a concept or skill and explain how it is similar to something else. The strength of this comparison can provide valuable insight into your students' thinking and reveal misconceptions or areas of confusion that you need to address. You can also share strong analogies with the class to help all students learn from one another.

Checking for Understanding Strategy 2: Engage in Error Analysis

Provide your students with a collection of problems or a work sample that contains errors. Individually, in pairs, or as a small group, students use what they have learned to try to identify the mistakes, correct them, and explain their corrections. You can ask students to explain (in writing or a video recording) how they knew the errors were present and how they went about fixing them.

Checking for Understanding Strategy 3: Rate Your Understanding

Ask students to evaluate their understanding of key concepts, processes, formulas, vocabulary, or skills, and provide a scale to rate their level of understanding. If you are working with secondary students, you can use a four-point, mastery-based scale (for example, 1—beginning, 2—developing, 3—proficient, and 4—mastery). If you work with younger learners, you can use an emoji scale with different facial expressions that align with how they are feeling about their level of understanding. This self-assessment can take place on paper or online using a digital form.

After the Learning: Encourage a Reflective Practice

At the end of a lesson, learning cycle, or unit, ask students to take time to reflect on their learning. This is critical to helping them appreciate the impact of the work they are doing on their content knowledge and skill set. If students recognize the value of their work, they are more likely to be motivated to engage in the learning (Pink, 2011).

You can use the following strategies—create sketchnotes, provide exit tickets, and use a then-and-now chart—to help your students reflect on their learning.

Reflecting on Learning Strategy 1: Create Sketchnotes

Sketchnotes are visual notes that encourage students to reflect on and share their learning in a visual format. Students can surface big ideas from a chapter, unit of study, or learning cycle with drawings and show their relationships in a free-form sketch that is not as restrictive as a concept map or flowchart. This visual reflection on learning provides insight into the students' learning and may present fewer barriers than a written explanation. Students can create sketchnotes on paper with colored pencils and markers, enjoying a more tactile experience, or they can use a digital program like Google Drawings (https://docs.google.com/drawings) or Canva (www .canva.com) to create their sketchnotes.

Reflecting on Learning Strategy 2: Provide Exit Tickets

The exit ticket, like the one mentioned in chapter 7 in the Evaluate section of the 5E instructional model (page 165), is a classic strategy that can enable you to quickly assess what students learned in a lesson. You can combine academic content questions with reflective questions to understand where students are in terms of their specific content knowledge or skill set and what they think they learned. Students can complete an exit ticket on paper or via a digital form. The beauty of using an online form to create your exit ticket and collect student responses is that you can quickly identify patterns in the data. This makes it more manageable to take what you've learned about your students to design the next lesson, building on what they know or circling back to review a concept or skill.

Reflecting on Learning Strategy 3: Use a Then-and-Now Chart

To understand the impact of a learning experience on a student, you can use a simple two-column then-and-now chart, pictured in figure 8.3 (page 182). This chart was inspired by the Project Zero's (2019b) "I Used to Think . . . Now I Think . . ."

Then	Now
Before beginning this lesson, unit, or learning cycle, I thought . . .	After engaging in this lesson, unit, or learning cycle, I think . . .
My thinking changed because . . .	
I'm still wondering . . .	

Source: Adapted from Project Zero, 2019b.

FIGURE 8.3: Then-and-now reflection chart.

*Visit **go.SolutionTree.com/technology** for a free reproducible version of this figure.*

thinking routine. First, ask students to describe what they knew, thought, believed, or could do before the lesson, unit, or learning cycle in the Then column. After listing items there, they can transition over to the Now column and describe what they know, think, believe, and can do now. Depending on the age of your students, you might ask them to compare the two columns in a short written explanation, or challenge them to describe which aspects of the lesson, unit, or learning cycle were most beneficial in helping them develop their understandings or skills.

Differentiation: Content, Process, and Product

Differentiation demands that we design with the specific needs of our learners in mind, and provide diverse groups of students with different ways to take in information and engage with the content, process that information and begin to make meaning, and demonstrate or share their learning (Tomlinson, 2017). As you collect informal data, you can use that information to identify where students are and what they need to continue making progress. What can you do within the design and facilitationof your lessons to more effectively meet students where they are in terms of their skills, abilities, needs, language proficiencies, and learning preferences? Following is some insight on differentiating the content, the process, and the product.

Differentiating the Content

Not all students will effectively access content in the same way. Differentiating the content means striving to present information in a format that is accessible for each student. One significant benefit of technology and online resources is the flexibility they offer students regarding *how* they access and engage with content. You can select texts at different Lexile levels to ensure students can access the information presented in writing. You can provide a text, video, and student-friendly podcast and allow students to decide whether reading, watching, or listening would be most effective. This choice will enable students to choose how they'll be most successful taking in this new information. Suppose you are using video to present information or model strategies. In that case, you might offer students the option to self-pace through a video lesson or join you for differentiated, teacher-led instruction. Additionally, you may want to provide additional demonstrations, examples, visuals, or models to aid students in understanding the information or skills you are presenting.

Differentiating the Process

Differentiating the process helps students make sense of the information or content. In a blended learning environment where student agency is a priority, you can offer options and allow students to choose a strategy that they believe will help them understand the information. You may want to provide students with the option to work independently, with a partner, or as part of a small group and let them decide which dynamic will be most beneficial.

You can provide tasks, practice problems, and writing prompts at different levels of rigor and complexity for students at various stages of readiness. As you design learning experiences for small groups and individual learners instead of for the whole class, it will be easier to pair activities with learners to ensure that it's within their zone of possibility. Additionally, adaptive software and online programs make differentiating the level of rigor and academic complexity more manageable.

As students work to make meaning, they may also benefit from various scaffolds and supports, like word banks or vocabulary videos, sentence frames, graphic organizers, mind maps, manipulatives, and guided note templates. These support structures can help students more successfully organize, think about, and make sense of what they are learning. You can use recorded video to assist students with additional modeling, vocabulary instruction, or support in developing the necessary background information to understand new concepts. Supports and scaffolds can be made available on paper or online, depending on a student's preference. Digital scaffolds may also increase accessibility because students can manipulate the text or video speed, and use features like voice to text.

In addition, you may want to consider allowing students to enjoy more control over the pace they work though the process of making meaning. Some students will benefit from more time on task, while others may not need as much time to create artifacts of their learning.

Differentiating the Product

Not all students will communicate and express their learning effectively in the same way. It is helpful to provide students with meaningful choices when it comes to demonstrating what they know or can do. You may want to consider giving students a collection of project structures or performance tasks in the form of a choice board. If they enjoy the agency to decide how they want to share their learning, you will more likely receive high-quality products that accurately reflect their understanding accurately.

You may want to build time into your work with students using blended learning models to create time and space to provide different levels of support as students work on these authentic forms of assessment. The level of feedback and support individual students will need to complete a task varies dramatically, but you want to support the process as they work on their products.

As you refine your approach to designing and facilitating blended learning experiences, remember that collecting informal formative assessment data is the best way to gauge what students know, can do, or need. These data can help you to make informed decisions about the models, instructional strategies, and technology tools you use to move students toward learning objectives. Without data, it is challenging to identify what students need and differentiate the content, process, or products to meet those needs.

As you refine your approach to designing and facilitating blended learning experiences, remember that collecting informal formative assessment data is the best way to gauge what students know, can do, or need. These data can help you to make informed decisions about the models, instructional strategies, and technology tools you use to move students toward learning objectives.

Approach Blended Learning With Balance in Mind

As you develop proficiency with blended learning models, it's essential to consider balance when designing learning experiences. Too often, teachers struggle with imbalance because this profession is so complex and multifaceted. Designing with a high level of intentionality can address many of the imbalances common in classrooms.

First, in too many classrooms, the teacher does the lion's share of the work in the lesson. Students, not the teacher, should put in the heavy cognitive effort of making meaning and applying their learning. This is why my definition of blended learning positions learners as dynamic agents. They cannot be passive consumers; they must be active participants. We must strive to design lessons that shift the locus of control from teacher to learner and create more balance in our lessons, so students are at the center of the learning.

When you approach the design of your lessons with balance in mind, what you are likely to get on the back end of your lesson will be more balanced too. For example, if teachers do not spend time designing a student-centered lesson but instead plan to spend a large chunk of the class period telling students what they know about a topic, little time is left in the lesson for students to engage with each other, wrestle with ideas, practice and apply, or engage in self- or peer assessment. That means students work in isolation without any teacher or peer support. The teacher is also likely to collect stacks of literal or digital work to take home to provide feedback on or grade because there was no time in class to complete these tasks.

Second, learning should be a balanced partnership between the teacher and the student. Students must share the responsibility for learning. That means they need to flex their metacognitive muscles by setting goals, tracking and monitoring their progress, reflecting on their learning, and assessing their work. These are critical skills students need to develop (often with teacher support) to become expert learners who are motivated, resourceful, strategic, and self-aware (Novak & Tucker, 2021). As students develop these essential skills, we can ask them to take a more active role in thinking about their learning and progress.

Third, technology should not be present to isolate learners and keep them quiet. Instead, you can harness the power of technology in a balanced way to cultivate a dynamic learning community capable of making meaning. Learning experiences that encourage conversation and collaboration among students are more likely to be engaging. They also help students view one another as valuable resources in the classroom. Instead of the teacher being the only source of information, support, or feedback, students develop the skills necessary to be resources for one another.

Review the lesson elements pictured in table 8.1 and consider the following questions.

- Which of these elements are typically balanced in my lessons? Which tend to be out of balance? For those elements that are often out of balance, how can I modify my design to correct those imbalances?

- How might balancing these aspects of my lesson yield a more engaging experience for myself and my students?

- What support might my students need to successfully drive their own learning and assume more responsibility in their learning? How can I provide skill building and support in these areas?

Table 8.1: Designing With Balance in Mind

Balancing the Elements Within a Lesson	
Teacher voice	Student voice
Online learning activities	Offline learning activities
Individual tasks	Collaborative tasks
Teacher feedback	Peer feedback
Teacher-controlled pacing	Student-controlled pacing
Teacher directed	Student agency and choice
Teacher dissemination of information	Student research, investigation, and discovery
Practice and review activities	Creative tasks
Teacher assessment	Self-assessment

If you design your lessons with a high level of intentionality and strive to balance the various elements within the lesson, there are several potential benefits.

- You will have more time to interact with and support individual or small groups of students to differentiate instruction, supports and scaffolds, practice, and application.

- Students will be more interested and engaged because they have more control over their learning.

- Students will develop their metacognitive and self-regulation skills.

- Students will learn how to be valuable resources for each other when it comes to feedback and collaboration.

- You will have more success building a dynamic learning community because students have more opportunities to learn with and from each other.

As you develop in your blended learning practice, you have an opportunity to re-evaluate your approach to designing and facilitating learning experiences to better meet the needs of diverse groups of students *and* lighten your workload. Instead of feeling pressure to do it all, strive to share the responsibility for learning with your students by designing lessons that encourage *them* to take an active role in the learning process.

Synchronous Versus Asynchronous Learning Activities

Blended learning weaves together online and offline learning, demanding thoughtful consideration of which learning activities would benefit from a synchronous versus an asynchronous mode. Table 8.2 (page 188) provides an overview of the differences between synchronous and asynchronous learning.

Synchronous activities benefit from human connection, social engagement, and teacher or peer support. Figure 8.4 (page 188) provides some different types of learning activities that work well in a synchronous mode. For example, student activities like building and maintaining relationships, receiving differentiated or personalized instruction and feedback, practicing and applying a new skill or strategy, engaging in a real-time discussion, or collaborating with classmates are more effective when students share a physical or virtual space. Access to the other members of the learning community enhances these learning activities.

Table 8.2: Synchronous Learning Versus Asynchronous Learning

Synchronous Learning	Asynchronous Learning
Student learning occurs at the same time and in the same place (for example, students are working in the classroom or meeting online for a video-conference session).	Student learning occurs at different times and in different places (for example, students are working remotely at home).
Students access content, resources, and activities at a specific time and in a particular location.	Students can access content, resources, and activities at any time, from anywhere.
Students *may* have some control over the pace of their learning, but they do not control the time or the place.	Students can control the time, place, and pace of their learning.
Students have access to teacher and peer support while completing assignments and tasks.	Students work independently to complete assignments and tasks.

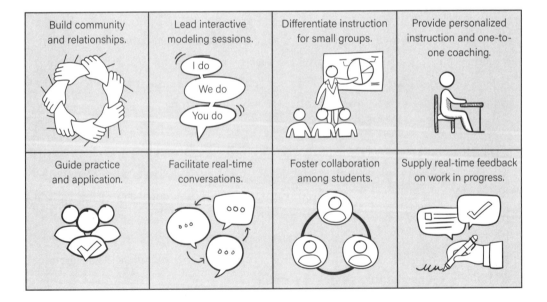

FIGURE 8.4: Synchronous learning activities.

By contrast, asynchronous activities benefit from learners enjoying a high degree of control over the time, place, and pace of their learning. Figure 8.5 provides some different types of learning activities that work well in an asynchronous mode.

FIGURE 8.5: Asynchronous learning activities.

For example, when students are engaging with new information in texts, videos, podcasts, or online resources, they are more likely to comprehend that new information if they can control the pace at which they consume and process it. Similarly, participation in text- or video-based online discussions works better with more time to process the question, articulate a response, and reply thoughtfully to peers.

Think Outside the Box: The Blended Learning Models Are Just a Starting Point

Don't view the blended learning models as an end point but rather a beginning. They provide a clear structure to help you shift from teacher-led, whole-group lessons to blended learning. The models are incredibly flexible and adaptable. Teachers often ask, "Am I doing this right?" or "Is this OK?" Try to avoid thinking about blended learning in black-and-white terms. There is no right or wrong. Feel free to bring your creativity to the design process.

The important takeaway from the examples in this section is that there is always room to grow in this work, which should keep your blended learning journey exciting and mentally stimulating. You can be as creative as you want with the design of these blended lessons. The sky is the limit!

When I work with teachers who have developed a high level of proficiency with one or more of the models, I'll suggest variations worth trying. There are two examples that stand out as especially useful. If teachers are using the station rotation model successfully, they can experiment with (1) a student-paced, free-flow station rotation or (2) a your-choice station rotation.

Student-Paced, Free-Flow Station Rotation

The student-paced, free-flow station rotation prioritizes student pacing. You break the class into groups, and each group begins at a particular station. However, instead of the teacher signaling the transition to the next station on a set schedule, you allow students to transition to the next station when *they* are ready. That way, the students control the pace at which they navigate tasks and move around the room. This design demands that the teacher-led station function more as a drop-in or feedback station to provide individual support on work in progress instead of instruction, which works better on a teacher-timed rotation. Teachers often worry about bottlenecks in the process, but in my experience they are rare. If they happen, you can give students the opportunity to move out of order or provide an overflow seating area if they anticipate that one station may require more time.

Your-Choice Station Rotation

Another variation on the station rotation is a your-choice station rotation. You can design a collection of stations (say, five or six total) and ask students to visit at least two or three of the stations during a rotation. You can use diagnostic or formative assessment data to identify at least one station at which each student would benefit from spending time. Students begin the rotation in these stations, which will function as their must-do stations. After they've completed that station, you can let them choose two may-do stations. The choice gives students the agency to decide where they would benefit from spending their time and energy during a lesson. This approach to the station rotation model makes the learning feel more personalized and relevant.

A your-choice station rotation works particularly well for a series of stations designed to help students review essential vocabulary, concepts, or skills in preparation for an assessment. It is also an excellent way to provide more personalized practice with skills or processes that students need more exposure to or time with. Another helpful way to use this strategy is to conclude a your-choice station rotation with an exit ticket that asks students to identify the stations they visited, provide a brief explanation for their choices, and briefly reflect on the experience and what they learned. This is an effective way to track where students spend their time during the your-choice station rotation.

Wrap-Up and Next Steps

Blended learning models provide much-needed direction and structure as you begin your blended learning journey. However, once you get comfortable with the basic design, there are additional layers you can add to increase the effectiveness of your blended lessons. You can build mechanisms into your lessons to collect formative assessment data to help you effectively differentiate the way students engage with the content, make meaning, and demonstrate their learning.

As you take your blended learning design to the next level, consider balancing the various elements in your lessons to more effectively share the responsibility of learning with your students. Consider incorporating more collaboration, peer feedback, and self-assessment to shift control over the learning to your students. That way, you are freed to work directly with individuals or small groups of learners and pull more time-consuming aspects of this work, like providing timely and actionable feedback, into the classroom.

The goal of this blended learning journey should be to free you to spend *more* time facilitating learning and engaging in the human side of teaching. Use the models and variations on them to accomplish the objective of spending more time working directly with your students. Remember, there is no right or wrong, and this is a journey that will take time.

Consider the following next steps to further your learning in this chapter and the book as a whole. See also the reflection questions on page 193.

- As you embark on this journey, I encourage you to visualize *what* you would like to see in your future classroom. Ponder the following questions.
    - ⌑ What scenes do you hope to create?
    - ⌑ How is the room set up, and how are students using the space?
    - ⌑ What are you doing? How are you using your class time? Where are you investing your finite time and energy?

- ¤ What are your students doing? How are they driving the learning?
- ¤ What qualities and characteristics are your students exhibiting?
- ¤ What do your students' interactions look like? How are they engaging with each other?

- Then, create a vision board of your future classroom. A vision board, like the one pictured in figure 6.3 (page 136) can help you make abstract ideas like blended learning, student engagement, and student-centered learning feel tangible and concrete. A vision board will also serve as a reminder of what you're working toward as you reflect on reading this book and experiment with the ideas, strategies, and models it describes.

Chapter 8: Taking Blended Learning to the Next Level—Reflect and Discuss

I encourage you to pause here to reflect on or discuss the following questions. If you are reading this book on your own, you can reflect on these questions in a blog post, publish your thoughts on your favorite social media platform, or capture your thoughts in a journal or notebook. If you are reading this book as part of a book club or book study, use the following questions to facilitate vibrant in-person or online discussions.

1. How often do you collect formative assessment data? Which formative assessment strategies do you typically use to assess prior knowledge, check for understanding, and encourage a reflective practice? How do you typically use the data you collect in your design work?

2. What form does differentiation tend to take in your lessons? In what ways do you differentiate how students access content, make meaning, or demonstrate their learning? Is there an area you would like to focus on developing? How? Have you used specific differentiation strategies that have been particularly useful or effective?

3. Review table 8.1 (page 186) about balancing elements in a blended lesson and identify areas you know you need to work on. Why is this aspect of the lesson typically out of balance? What pressures are at work causing this imbalance? How might you use blended learning models to try to create more balance in this area? What skills might you need to help students develop to bring these elements into balance?

4. Review table 8.1 (page 186) about balancing elements in a blended lesson and identify an area you feel you do a good job balancing. Why do you think you can keep these elements in balance? What beliefs about learning made keeping these elements in balance a priority for you?

5. How have you decided when to have students work synchronously versus asynchronously? When reading that section of this chapter, what realizations or thoughts did you have about your current approach? Moving forward, how can you use the suggestions in this chapter to more intentionally pair the learning task with the best mode?

6. Why do you think it is important to view the blended learning models as a starting point instead of an end point? How might this perspective impact your engagement with blended learning over time? What impact might playing with variations on the models have on your students' level of engagement over time?

CONCLUSION

When I wrote my first book on blended learning in 2011, I shared what I had learned in the early stages of my blended learning journey. My early experimentations, failures, lessons, and resources I developed to support my students composed the bulk of that book. It reflected my initial excitement about the potential of using technology and online resources to engage students in active learning with their peers.

As a teacher, coach, trainer, and professor, I have learned much from my work about designing, instructing, and facilitating learning in blended and online learning environments. The goal of this blend is to shift students to the center of the learning process. That does not make blended learning a threat to the vital work that teachers do. Instead, it should free you to spend more time on the aspects of this work that you find rewarding and fulfilling.

This book reflects my belief that blended learning is better for teachers and students. Technology isn't going anywhere, so like every other industry, educators must learn to leverage technology to make learning more engaging, relevant, accessible, and equitable. At some point, all learning will be some form of blended learning. The piece you have control over is whether the addition of technology isolates learners or facilitates more human interactions and connections. I hope this book will support you as you pursue the latter. In service of that, I have some final points of advice to share before you set out on this journey.

Advice as You Shift to Blended Learning

As you embark on your blended learning journey, I would like to share the following words of advice. This advice is born from the lessons I've learned. I hope these reminders provide you with some perspective as you reimagine your work and the experiences you want your students to have in class and online.

Reminder 1: Think Big, Start Small—Build on Small Wins

It's easy to get excited about the potential of blended learning (or anything new, for that matter) and try to do too much at once. However, your transition from designing and facilitating teacher-led, whole-group lessons to blended learning experiences will take time. You are more likely to stay excited and engaged if you build on a series of small wins.

I suggest starting with a single blended learning model, like the station rotation model or the whole-group rotation model. As you design your first lesson, make sure that most of the activities you ask students to do are familiar to them. That way, your students can acclimate to the rotation without feeling pressure to navigate new technology tools or unfamiliar tasks. In these early stages of implementation, you do not need to push yourself to differentiate or provide students with agency in every lesson or station. Instead, you can build up to that when you and your students are comfortable with the structure and have a couple of successful rotations under your belts.

Reminder 2: Cultivate a Growth Mindset, and Use the Word *Yet*

Cultivating a growth mindset isn't just for students. You can also grow, develop, and improve with hard work, dedication, and practice (Dweck, 2015). You may not feel particularly confident using technology (*yet*) or designing learning experiences using a particular blended learning model (*yet*), but that does not mean you cannot develop your proficiency and confidence in these areas. Give yourself the space and grace to learn.

Reminder 3: Design Learning Experiences That Free You From the Front of the Room and Allow You to Facilitate Learning

Despite the immense pressure we are under to cover content, the most rewarding aspect of teaching is our interactions with students. When we can sit alongside individuals or small groups of learners, we can more effectively meet their specific needs and support their individual development and progress. As you work with these models, use them to create the time and space necessary to act as a coach, facilitating student learning.

Facilitation might take the form of real-time feedback sessions, teacher-guided, small-group discussions, or conferencing sessions focused on discussing student progress. These moments when you are working directly with an individual or small group of students necessitate that the class is engaged in learning without you needing to orchestrate the experience. If you shift the transfer of information and modeling sessions online using video, design collaborative small-group tasks that provide peer support, and provide the necessary scaffolds to support independent work, then you will have more time to engage with learners. Technology is no match for the human side of teaching. But we can lean on technology to create space for human connection in our classrooms and online.

Reminder 4: Prioritize Student Agency to Remove Barriers and Provide Flexible Pathways

Our classrooms comprise learners with different skills, abilities, needs, interests, learning preferences, and language proficiencies. As a result, a single pathway will rarely move all students toward a firm learning goal or objective. Instead, we must design with a high level of intentionality by identifying potential barriers to accessing the information or fully engaging in a learning activity.

For example, if you want to engage the class in a discussion about a text, topic, or reading, some students will be comfortable jumping into a real-time conversation, while other students will feel anxious or shy or need more time to process the question. They might prefer to engage in an online text- or video-based discussion. If we strive to identify potential barriers in our design work, we can proactively work to mitigate or eliminate them by building student agency and meaningful choice into the lesson or learning experience. When we give students agency in the lesson, we invite them to identify a path that will work for them.

Reminder 5: Embrace Your Role as the Lead Learner in the Classroom

As the lead learner in your classroom, your students will benefit from seeing you try new models, strategies, and technology tools. If your lessons don't go smoothly, invite your students into the conversation about how you might improve the experience in the future. This openness creates a class culture where *everyone* is learning. When students see you working outside of your comfort zone and experimenting, it is a lot less scary for them to take risks or make mistakes. It reinforces your partnership with learners when they see that you are also committed to learning.

As the lead learner, you need to be curious about what is working and what needs revision or reimagining. If you regularly collect feedback from your students, you can learn from them and use their insight to continually improve their experiences. The most exciting part of this journey for me has been my realization that there is *always* more to learn. There is no end point. There is always space to stretch and grow.

On Your Way

So, as you embark on your blended learning journey, give yourself permission to experiment, fail, and grow. Remember that hitting bumps and failing is simply part of any learning journey. When you encounter a challenge or roadblock, use that as an opportunity to reflect and revamp your approach. Lean on your colleagues or your collaborative team in these moments to access the support and inspiration you need to keep moving forward.

GLOSSARY

Adaptive software. Software designed to adjust the level of rigor based on the user's performance to provide a personalized experience.

Asynchronous learning. Learning that takes place at different times and from different places; ideal for learning that benefits from a high degree of student control over the time, place, and pace of learning.

Blended learning. Active, engaged learning online combined with active, engaged learning offline to give students more control over the time, place, pace, and path of their learning.

Cognitive presence. The learner's ability "to construct and confirm meaning through sustained reflection and discourse in a critical community of inquiry" (Garrison et al., 2001, p. 11) grounded in the practical inquiry model.

Community of inquiry (COI) framework. A framework composed of the social, cognitive, and teaching presences and grounded in the construct of collaborative constructivism, or the belief that individuals construct meaning and that meaning is validated in collaboration with others via discourse, reflection, and social collaboration (Garrison & Archer, 2000; Vaughan, 2010).

Crowdsource. To allow members of the class, or the crowd, to generate and share information and ideas.

Differentiation. A proactive approach to design to ensure the task is appropriate for the specific learner or group of learners. It strives to meet students where they are in their learning journeys so everyone can be successful in making progress toward mastering the learning objectives (Tomlinson, 2017).

Social presence. Learners' ability to project their social and emotional selves in an online or blended learning environment for the purpose of establishing trust and inviting open communication (Garrison & Vaughan, 2008; Swan, 2019).

Student agency. Students' ability to make key decisions about their learning experience.

Student engagement. Students' affective or emotional reaction, behavioral or academic and social response, and cognitive response or investment of mental energy and focus in the learning activities and peer interactions (Borup, West, Graham, & Davies, 2014).

Synchronous learning. Learning that takes place in real time in a shared physical or virtual space; ideal for learning that benefits from social interaction, peer support, or interactions with a learning community.

Teacher engagement. A motivational construct that reflects teachers' choices to dedicate energy resources to their work and that is composed of cognitive engagement, emotional engagement, social engagement with students, and social engagement with colleagues (Klassen, Yerdelen, & Durksen, 2013).

Teaching presence. The design, facilitation, and direction of the cognitive and social presences in a course to yield high-quality learning; the "binding element" of the community of inquiry framework (Garrison et al., 1999, p. 96; Swan, 2019).

Zone of possibility. A spin on Vygotsky's (1978) zone of proximal development that describes a task within students' ability to complete on their own or with peer support.

REFERENCES AND RESOURCES

Akyol, Z., & Garrison, D. R. (2011). Understanding cognitive presence in an online and blended community of inquiry: Assessing outcomes and processes for deep approaches to learning. *British Journal of Educational Technology, 42*(2), 233–250. Accessed at http://dx.doi.org/10.1111/j.1467-8535.2009.01029.x on November 23, 2021.

Ausubel, D. P. (2012). *The acquisition and retention of knowledge: A cognitive view.* New York: Springer Science & Business Media.

Baas, D., Castelijns, J., Vermeulen, M., Martens, R., & Segers, M. (2015). The relation between assessment for learning and elementary students' cognitive and metacognitive strategy use. *British Journal of Educational Psychology, 85*(1), 33–46.

Bazzano, A. N., Anderson, C. E., Hylton, C., & Gustat, J. (2018). Effect of mindfulness and yoga on quality of life for elementary school students and teachers: Results of a randomized controlled school-based study. *Psychology Research and Behavior Management, 11*, 81–89.

Berliner, W. (2020, January 28). *"Schools are killing curiosity": Why we need to stop telling children to shut up and learn.* Accessed at www.theguardian.com/education/2020/jan/28/schools-killing-curiosity-learn on February 28, 2022.

Blackburn, B. (2018). *Productive struggle is a learner's sweet spot.* Accessed at www.ascd.org/ascd-express/vol14/num11/productive-struggle-is-a-learners-sweet-spot.aspx on February 3, 2021.

Borup, J., Graham, C. R., & Drysdale, J. S. (2014). The nature of teacher engagement at an online high school. *British Journal of Educational Technology, 45*(5), 793–806. Accessed at http://dx.doi.org/10.1111/bjet.12089 on November 23, 2021.

Borup, J., West, R. E., Graham, C. R., & Davies, R. S. (2014). The adolescent community of engagement framework: A lens for research on K–12 online learning. *Journal of Technology and Teacher Education, 22*(1), 107–129. Accessed at www.editlib.org/p/112371 on March 2, 2022.

Brame, C. (2015). *Effective educational videos.* Accessed at https://cft.vanderbilt.edu/guides-sub-pages/effective-educational-videos on February 21, 2022.

Braund, H., & DeLuca, C. (2018). Elementary students as active agents in their learning: An empirical study of the connections between assessment practices and student metacognition. *Australian Educational Researcher: Special Issue on Student Agency in Classroom Assessment, 45*(1), 65–85.

Bray, B., & McClaskey, K. (2014). *Make learning personal: The what, who, wow, where, and why.* Thousand Oaks, CA: Corwin Press.

Breivik, J. (2016). Critical thinking in online educational discussions measured as progress through inquiry phases: A discussion of the cognitive presence construct in the community of inquiry framework. *International Journal of E-Learning & Distance Education, 31*(1), 1.

Brown, B. (2010). *The power of vulnerability* [Video file]. Accessed at www.ted.com/talks /brene_brown_the_power_of_vulnerability on December 8, 2021.

Bruner, J. S., Goodnow, J. J., & Austin, G.A. (1956). *A study of thinking.* London, UK: Chapman & Hall.

Bybee, R. W. (2014). The BSCS 5E instructional model: Personal reflections and contemporary implications. *Science and Children, 51*(8), 10–13.

Bybee, R. W., Taylor, J. A., Gardner, A., Van Scotter, P., Powell, J. C., Westbrook, A., & Landes, N. (2006). *The BSCS 5E Instructional Model: Origins and effectiveness.* Accessed at https://bscs.org/reports/the-bscs-5e-instructional-model-origins-and -effectiveness on April 11, 2022.

Cohen, R. K., Opatosky, D. K., Savage, J., Stevens, S. O., & Darrah, E. P. (2021). *The metacognitive student: How to teach academic, social, and emotional intelligence in every content area.* Bloomington, IN: Solution Tree Press.

Collaborative for Academic, Social, and Emotional Learning. (n.d.). *What is the CASEL framework?: A framework creates a foundation for applying evidence-based SEL strategies to your community.* Accessed at https://casel.org/fundamentals-of-sel/what-is-the-casel -framework on December 9, 2021.

Cregg, D. R., & Cheavens, J. S. (2021). Gratitude interventions: Effective self-help? A meta-analysis of the impact on symptoms of depression and anxiety. *Journal of Happiness Studies, 22*(1), 413–445.

DuFour, R., DuFour, R., Eaker, R., Many, T., & Mattos, M. (2016). *Learning by doing: A handbook for Professional Learning Communities at Work®* (3rd ed.). Bloomington, IN: Solution Tree Press.

Dweck, C. (2015). Carol Dweck revisits the "growth mindset." Accessed at www.edweek .org/leadership/opinion-carol-dweck-revisits-the-growth-mindset/2015/09 on November 23, 2021.

Elmahdi, I., Al-Hattami, A., & Fawzi, H. (2018). Using technology for formative assessment to improve students' learning. *Turkish Online Journal of Educational Technology (TOJET)*, *17*(2), 182–188.

Ferdiansyah, S., Ridho, M. A., Sembilan, F. D., & Zahro, S. F. (2020). Online literature circles during the COVID-19 pandemic: Engaging undergraduate students in Indonesia. *TESOL Journal*, *11*(3). Accessed at https://doi.org/10.1002/tesj.544 on March 1, 2022.

Fisher, D., & Frey, N. (2014). *Better learning through structured teaching: A framework for the gradual release of responsibility* (2nd ed.). Alexandria, VA: Association for Supervision and Curriculum Development.

Frayer, D. A., Frederick, W. C., & Klausmeier, H. G. (1969). *A schema for testing the level of concept mastery* (Technical Report no. 16). Madison: University of Wisconsin.

Garrison, D. R., & Archer, W. (2000). A transactional perspective on teaching and learning: A framework for adult and higher education. New York: Elsevier.

Garrison, D. R., & Vaughan, N. D. (2008). *Blended learning in higher education: Framework, principles, and guidelines.* Hoboken, NJ: Wiley.

Garrison, D. R., Anderson, T., & Archer, W. (1999). Critical inquiry in a text-based environment: Computer conferencing in higher education. *The Internet and Higher Education*, *2*(2–3), 87–105. Accessed at http://dx.doi.org/10.1016/S1096 -7516(00)00016-6 on November 23, 2021.

Garrison, D. R., Anderson, T., & Archer, W. (2001). Critical thinking, cognitive presence, and computer conferencing in distance education. *American Journal of Distance Education*, *15*(1), 7–23. Accessed at http://dx.doi.org/10.1080/08923640109527071 on November 23, 2021.

Garrison, D. R., Anderson, T., & Archer, W. (2010). The first decade of the community of inquiry framework: A retrospective. *The Internet and Higher Education*, *13*(1–2), 5–9. Accessed at http://dx.doi.org/10.1016/j.iheduc.2009.10.003 on November 24, 2021.

Gebre, E., Saroyan, A., & Bracewell, R. (2014). Students' engagement in technology-rich classrooms and its relationship to professors' conceptions of effective teaching. *British Journal of Educational Technology*, *45*(1), 83–96.

Grafwallner, P. (2021). *Not yet . . . and that's OK: How productive struggle fosters student learning.* Bloomington, IN: Solution Tree Press.

Guo, P. J., Kim, J., & Rubin, R. (2014, March). How video production affects student engagement: An empirical study of MOOC videos. In M. Sahami (Ed.), *Proceedings of the First ACM Conference on Learning @ Scale Conference* (pp. 41–50). New York: Association for Computing Machinery.

Hamilton, E. R., Rosenberg, J. M., & Akcaoglu, M. (2016). The substitution augmentation modification redefinition (SAMR) model: A critical review and suggestions for its use. *TechTrends*, *60*(5), 433–441.

Han, M., & Hamilton, E. R. (2021). Promoting engagement and learning: Using the fishbowl strategy in online and hybrid college courses. *College Teaching*, 1–9.

Hastie, P. A., Rudisill, M. E., & Wadsworth, D. D. (2013). Providing students with voice and choice: Lessons from intervention research on autonomy-supportive climates in physical education. *Sport, Education and Society*, *18*(1), 38–56.

Hattie, J., & Timperley, H. (2007). The power of feedback. *Review of Educational Research*, *77*(1), 81–112.

Hematian, F., Rezaei, A. M., & Mohammadyfar, M. A. (2017). On the effect of goal setting on self-directed learning, achievement motivation, and academic achievement among students. *Modern Applied Science*, *11*(1), 37–47.

Heritage, M. (2013). *Formative assessment in practice: A process of inquiry and action*. Cambridge, MA: Harvard Education Press.

Jang, H., Kim, E. J., & Reeve, J. (2012). Longitudinal test of self-determination theory's motivation mediation model in a naturally occurring classroom context. *Journal of Educational Psychology*, *104*(4), 1175–1188. Accessed at https://doi.org/10.1037/a0028089 on November 24, 2021.

Kazakoff, E. R., Macaruso, P., & Hook, P. (2018). Efficacy of a blended learning approach to elementary school reading instruction for students who are english learners. *Educational Technology Research and Development: A Bi-Monthly Publication of the Association for Educational Communications & Technology*, *66*(2), 429–449. Accessed at https://doi.org/10.1007/s11423-017-9565-7 on March 2, 2022.

Kilbane, C. R., & Milman, N. B. (2014). *Teaching models: Designing instruction for 21st century learners*. Boston: Pearson.

Klassen, R. M., Yerdelen, S., & Durksen, T. L. (2013). Measuring teacher engagement: Development of the engaged teachers scale (ETS). *Frontline Learning Research*, *1*(2), 33–52. Accessed at http://dx.doi.org/10.14786/flr.v1i2.44 on November 24, 2021.

Kreijns, K., Van Acker, F., Vermeulen, M., & Van Buuren, H. (2014). Community of inquiry: Social presence revisited. *E-Learning and Digital Media*, *11*(1), 5–18.

Kress, J. S., & Elias, M. J. (2020). *Nurturing students' character: Everyday teaching activities for social-emotional learning*. New York: Routledge.

Kundu, A., Bej, T., & Rice, M. (2021). Time to engage: Implementing math and literacy blended learning routines in an Indian elementary classroom. *Education and Information Technologies*, *26*(1), 1201–1220.

Lawson, H. A., & Lawson, M. A. (2020). Student engagement and disengagement as a collective action problem. *Education Sciences, 10*(8), 212.

Lipman, M. (2003). *Thinking in education* (2nd ed.). Cambridge, UK: Cambridge University Press.

Matriano, E. A. (2020). Ensuring student-centered, constructivist and project-based experiential learning applying the exploration, research, interaction and creation (ERIC) learning model. *International Online Journal of Education and Teaching, 7*(1), 214–227.

McCallum, S., Schultz, J., Sellke, K., & Spartz, J. (2015). An examination of the flipped classroom approach on college student academic involvement. *International Journal of Teaching and Learning in Higher Education, 27*(1), 42–55.

McTighe, J., & Wiggins, G. (2013). *Essential questions: Opening doors to student understanding.* Alexandria, VA: Association for Supervision and Curriculum Development.

McTighe, J., Doubet, K. J., & Carbaugh, E. M. (2020). *Designing authentic performance tasks and projects: Tools for meaningful learning and assessment.* Alexandria, VA: Association for Supervision and Curriculum Development.

Mehta, R., & Aguilera, E. (2020). A critical approach to humanizing pedagogies in online teaching and learning. *The International Journal of Information and Learning Technology, 37*(3), 109–120. Accessed at www.researchgate.net/publication /340695293_A_critical_approach_to_humanizing_pedagogies_in_online_teaching _and_learning on November 24, 2021.

Meier, B. S., & Rossi, K. A. (2020). Removing instructional barriers with UDL. *Kappa Delta Pi Record, 56*(2), 82–88.

Mikel, B. (2020). How Brené Brown runs emotionally intelligent Zoom meetings. Accessed at www.inc.com/betsy-mikel/how-brene-brown-runs-emotionally-intelligent -zoom-meetings.html on November 24, 2021.

The New Teacher Project. (2018). *The opportunity myth: What students can show us about how school is letting them down—And how to fix it.* Accessed at https:// opportunitymyth.tntp.org on November 23, 2021.

Nottage, C., & Morse, V. (2021). *Independent investigation method teaching research skills in grades K–12 revised for 2012: College and career readiness skills aligned with CCSS and TEKS.* New York: Routledge.

Novak, K., & Tucker, C. R. (2021). *UDL and blended learning: Thriving in flexible learning landscapes.* San Diego, CA: IMpress.

Partnership for 21st Century Learning. (2019). *Framework for 21st century learning definitions.* Accessed at http://static.battelleforkids.org/documents/p21/P21 _Framework_DefinitionsBFK.pdf on January 11, 2022.

Patall, E. A., Pituch, K. A., Steingut, R. R., Vasquez, A. C., Yates, N., & Kennedy, A. A. U. (2019). Agency and high school science students' motivation, engagement, and classroom support experiences. *Journal of Applied Developmental Psychology, 62,* 77–92.

Patrick, S., Kennedy, K., & Powell, A. (2013). *Mean what you say: Defining and integrating personalized, blended and competency education.* Vienna, VA: Aurora Institute.

Pearson, P. D., & Gallagher, M. C. (1983). The instruction of reading comprehension. *Contemporary Educational Psychology, 8*(3), 317–344.

Pegrum, M., Oakley, G., & Faulkner, R. (2013). Schools going mobile: A study of the adoption of mobile handheld technologies in Western Australian independent schools. *Australasian Journal of Educational Technology, 29*(1), 66–81. Accessed at http://dx.doi .org/10.14742/ajet.64 on March 2, 2022.

Pink, D. H. (2011). *Drive: The surprising truth about what motivates us.* New York: Penguin.

Postholm, M. B. (2013). Classroom management: What does research tell us? *European Educational Research Journal, 12*(3), 389–402.

Pressley, T. (2021). Factors contributing to teacher burnout during COVID-19. *Educational Researcher,* 50(5), 325–327. Accessed at https://journals.sagepub.com/doi /full/10.3102/0013189X211004138 on March 2, 2022.

Project Zero. (2019a). *Connect, extend, challenge.* Accessed at https://pz.harvard.edu/sites /default/files/Connect%20Extend%20Challenge_1.pdf on December 2, 2021.

Project Zero. (2019b). *I used to think . . . now I think . . .: A routine for reflecting on how and why our thinking has changed.* Accessed at http://www.pz.harvard.edu/sites/default /files/I%20Used%20to%20Think%20-%20Now%20I%20Think_1.pdf on March 1, 2022.

Project Zero. (2019c). *See/think/wonder: A thinking routine for exploring works of art and other interesting things.* Accessed at https://pz.harvard.edu/sites/default/files/See%20 Think%20Wonder.pdf on December 2, 2021.

Project Zero. (2019d). *Who am I? Explore, connect, identify, belong.* Accessed at https:// pz.harvard.edu/sites/default/files/Who%20Am%20I%20-%20Exploring%20 Complexity.pdf on November 24, 2021.

Puentedura, R. R. (2013, May 29). *SAMR: Moving from enhancement to transformation* [Blog post]. Accessed at www.hippasus.com/rrpweblog/archives/000095.html on November 24, 2021.

Reckmeyer, M. (2019, October 30). *Focus on student engagement for better academic outcomes.* Accessed at www.gallup.com/education/267521/focus-student-engagement -better-academic-outcomes.aspx on February 28, 2022.

Roessger, K. M., Daley, B. J., & Hafez, D. A. (2018). Effects of teaching concept mapping using practice, feedback, and relational framing. *Learning and Instruction*, *54*, 11–21.

Roth, G., Assor, A., Kanat-Maymon, Y., & Kaplan, H. (2007). Autonomous motivation for teaching: How self-determined teaching may lead to self-determined learning. *Journal of Educational Psychology*, *99*(4), 761–774. Accessed at http://dx.doi.org /10.1037/0022-0663.99.4.761 on November 24, 2021.

Ryan, R. M., & Deci, E. L. (2019). Brick by brick: The origins, development, and future of self-determination theory. In A. Elliot (Ed.), *Advances in motivation science* (Vol. 6, pp. 111–156). Amsterdam, Netherlands: Elsevier.

Sahni, J. (2019). Does blended learning enhance student engagement? Evidence from higher education. *Journal of E-learning and Higher Education*. Accessed at https:// ibimapublishing.com/articles/JELHE/2019/121518 on March 2, 2022.

Schawbel, D. (2013). Brené Brown: How vulnerability can make our lives better. Accessed at www.forbes.com/sites/danschawbel/2013/04/21/brene-brown-how-vulnerability -can-make-our-lives-better on November 24, 2021.

Schimmer, T. (2016). *Grading from the inside out: Bringing accuracy to student assessment through a standards-based mindset*. Bloomington, IN: Solution Tree Press.

Schmitt, M. T., Branscombe, N. R., Postmes, T., & Garcia, A. (2014). The consequences of perceived discrimination for psychological well-being: A meta-analytic review. *Psychological Bulletin*, *140*(4), 921–948.

Schneider, S., Nebel, S., Beege, M., & Rey, G. D. (2018). The autonomy-enhancing effects of choice on cognitive load, motivation and learning with digital media. *Learning and Instruction*, *58*, 161–172.

Sekeres, M. J., Bonasia, K., St-Laurent, M., Pishdadian, S., Winocur, G., Grady, C., et al. (2016). Recovering and preventing loss of detailed memory: Differential rates of forgetting for detail types in episodic memory. *Learning & Memory*, *23*(2), 72–82.

Shemshack, A., & Spector, J. M. (2020). A systematic literature review of personalized learning terms. *Smart Learning Environments*, *7*(1), 1–20.

Sinek, S. (2009). *Start with why: How great leaders inspire everyone to take action*. New York: Penguin.

Song, L., Singleton, E. S., Hill, J. R., & Koh, M. H. (2004). Improving online learning: Student perceptions of useful and challenging characteristics. *The Internet and Higher Education*, *7*(1), 59–70.

Sparks, S. (2013). *Students can learn by explaining, studies say*. Accessed at www.edweek.org /leadership/students-can-learn-by-explaining-studies-say/2013/05 on February 28, 2022.

Spurlock, M. (Director). (2004). *Super size me* [Film]. The Con.

Staker, H., & Horn, M. B. (2012). *Classifying K–12 blended learning.* Mountain View, CA: Innosight Institute. Accessed at www.christenseninstitute.org/wp-content/uploads /2013/04/Classifying-K-12-blended-learning.pdf on November 24, 2021.

Standford Teaching Commons. (n.d.). *Inclusive and equitable discussions.* Accessed at https://teachingcommons.stanford.edu/explore-teaching-guides/inclusive-teaching -guide/learning-activities/inclusive-and-equitable on March 1, 2022.

Stasiak, L. W. (2017). *Stress, anxiety, and social emotional learning in education: Perceptions of undergraduate, pre service, and practicing teachers* [Doctoral dissertation, Lesley University]. Accessed at www.proquest.com/docview/1882289368 on November 24, 2021.

Sukardjo, M., & Salam, M. (2020). Effect of concept attainment models and self-directed Learning (SDL) on mathematics learning outcomes. *International Journal of Instruction, 13*(3), 275–292.

Susanna, S., Herliana, F., Elisa, E., Farhan, A., Rizal, S., & Musdar, M. (2021). The effect of self-regulation and motivation to outcomes learning using blended learning approach. *Turkish Journal of Computer and Mathematics Education, 12*(6), 4226–4233.

Swan, K. (2019). Social construction of knowledge and the community of inquiry framework. In I. Jung (Ed.), *Open and distance education theory revisited: Implications for a digital era* (pp. 57–66). Singapore: Springer.

Terada, Y. (2020, May 4). A powerful model for understanding good tech integration. Accessed at www.edutopia.org/article/powerful-model-understanding-good-tech -integration on November 24, 2021.

Tomlinson, C. A. (2017). *How to differentiate instruction in academically diverse classrooms* (3rd ed.). Alexandria, VA: Association for Supervision and Curriculum Development.

Townsley, M., & Wear, N. L. (2020). *Making grades matter: Standards-based grading in a secondary PLC at Work.* Bloomington, IN: Solution Tree Press.

Truitt, A. A., & Ku, H. Y. (2018). A case study of third grade students' perceptions of the station rotation blended learning model in the United States. *Educational Media International, 55*(2), 153–169.

Tucker, C. (2012). *Blended learning in grades 4–12: Leveraging the power of technology to create student-centered classrooms.* Thousand Oaks, CA: Corwin Press.

Tucker, C. R. (2020a). *Balance with blended learning: Partner with your students to reimagine learning and reclaim your life.* Thousand Oaks, CA: Corwin Press.

Tucker, C. R. (2020b). *Teacher engagement in high school full-release blended learning courses.* [Doctoral dissertation, Pepperdine University]. Accessed at www.proquest.com/open view/987c8516f8be1085afe1bef6899bd1ed/1?pq-origsite=gscholar&cbl=44156 on November 24, 2021.

Tucker, C. R. (2021a). Innovating inside the box with George Couros [Podcast]. *The Balance*. Accessed at https://podcasts.apple.com/us/podcast/innovating-inside-the-box -with-george-couros/id1485751335?i=1000523909568 on November 24, 2021.

Tucker, C. R. (2021b). Reclaiming personalized learning with Paul France [Podcast]. *The Balance*. Accessed at https://podcasts.apple.com/us/podcast/reclaiming-personalized -learning-with-paul-france/id1485751335?i=1000534012808 on November 24, 2021.

Tucker, C. R., Wycoff, T., & Green, J. T. (2017). *Blended learning in action: A practical guide toward sustainable change*. Thousand Oaks, CA: Corwin Press.

Turner, J., Young-Lowe, W., & Newton, J. (2018). Teachers' perceptions of the use of blended learning for instructional delivery and student production in K–12 classrooms. *International Journal of Learning and Development*, 8(2), 18–26.

Vago, D. R., & Silbersweig, D. A. (2012). *Self-awareness, self-regulation, and self-transcendance (S-ART): A framework for understanding the neurobiological mechanisms of mindfulness*. Accessed at www.frontiersin.org/articles/10.3389/fnhum.2012.00296/full on February 28, 2022.

Van de Weijer-Bergsma, E., Langenberg, G., Brandsma, R., Oort, F. J., & Bögels, S. M. (2012). The effectiveness of a school-based mindfulness training as a program to prevent stress in elementary school children. *Mindfulness*, 5(3), 238–248.

Vaughan, N. D. (2010). A blended community of inquiry approach: Linking student engagement and course redesign. *The Internet and Higher Education*, 13(1–2), 60–65. Accessed at http://dx.doi.org/10.1016/j.iheduc.2009.10.007 on March 2, 2022.

Vaughan, N. D., Cleveland-Innes, M., & Garrison, D. R. (2013). *Teaching in blended learning environments*. Edmonton, Alberta, Canada: Athabasca Universtiy Press.

Verkuyten, M., Thijs, J. T., & Gharaei, N. (2019). Discrimination and academic (dis) engagement of ethnic-racial minority students: A social identity threat perspective. *Social Psychology of Education*, 22(2), 267–290.

Vygotsky, L. S. (1978). *Mind in society: The development of higher psychological processes*. Cambridge, MA: Harvard University Press.

Walkup, J. R., & Squire, S. (2020). *The art and science of lesson design: Practical approaches to boosting cognitive rigor in the classroom*. Lanham, MD: Rowman & Littlefield.

Wisniewski, B., Zierer, K., & Hattie, J. (2020). *The power of feedback revisited: A meta-analysis of educational feedback research*. Accessed at https://doi.org/10.3389/fpsyg .2019.03087 on February 22, 2022.

Yang, H. H., Zhu, S., & MacLeod, J. (2016, July). Collaborative teaching approaches: Extending current blended learning models. In S. K. S. Cheung, L.-F. Kwok, J. Shang, A. Wang, & R. Kwan (Eds.), *Blending Learning: Aligning Theory With Practices—9th International Conference* (pp. 49–59). Cham, Switzerland: Springer.

INDEX

Creating the Anywhere, Anytime Classroom
Casey Reason, Lisa Reason, and Crystal Guiler
Discover the steps K–12 educators must take to facilitate online learning and maximize student growth using digital tools. Each chapter includes suggestions and examples tied to pedagogical practices associated with learning online, so you can confidently engage in the best practices with your students.
BKF772

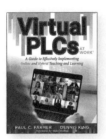

Virtual PLCs at Work
Paul C. Farmer and Dennis King
Explore an abundance of tools, tips, and best practices for remote teacher collaboration in virtual professional learning communities. Learn how to implement online professional learning communities in a way that maintains the power of the PLC process to ensure learning for all.
BKG028

Capturing the Classroom
Ellen I. Linnihan
Harness the power of video to cultivate equity, create stability, and reach students any time. With *Capturing the Classroom*, you will learn concrete and doable ways to record lectures, classroom discussions, tutorials, review sessions, and more to support any content area or curriculum.
BKF998

Shifting to Digital
James A. Bellanca, Gwendolyn Battle Lavert, and Kate Bellanca
Rely on *Shifting to Digital* to give you clear, concise, and helpful answers to all of your remote teaching questions. This comprehensive guide provides specific strategies for planning high-engagement instruction, handling technology, assessing collaboration and assignments, and more.
BKG006

Visit SolutionTree.com or call 800.733.6786 to order.

Wait! Your professional development journey doesn't have to end with the last pages of this book.

We realize improving student learning doesn't happen overnight. And your school or district shouldn't be left to puzzle out all the details of this process alone.

No matter where you are on the journey, we're committed to helping you get to the next stage.

Take advantage of everything from **custom workshops** to **keynote presentations** and **interactive web and video conferencing**. We can even help you develop an action plan tailored to fit your specific needs.

Let's get the conversation started.

Call 888.763.9045 today.

SolutionTree.com